Expertise
and the
Primary School Teacher

Expertise and the Primary School Teacher

PHILIP H. TAYLOR

NFER-NELSON

Published by The NFER-NELSON Publishing Company Ltd.,
Darville House, 2 Oxford Road East,
Windsor, Berkshire SL4 1DF

and in the United States of America by

NFER-NELSON, 242 Cherry Street, Philadelphia, PA 19106 – 1906.
Tel: (215) 238 0939. Telex: 244489.

First Published 1986
© 1986 Philip H. Taylor

Library of Congress Cataloging in Publication data

Taylor, Philip Hampson.
  Expertise and the primary school teacher.
  Bibliography: p.
  Includes index.
  1. Elementary school teaching — Great Britain — Evaluation. 2.
Elementary school teachers — Great Britain. 3. Education, Elementary —
Great Britain — Curricula. I. Title.
LB1555.T26 1986 372.11'00941 86–5219
ISBN 0–7005–1036–2

Photoset in Times by David John (Services) Ltd., Maidenhead, Berks.

Printed in Great Britain by A. Wheaton & Co., Ltd., Exeter

ISBN 0 7005 1036 2
Code 8234 02 1

Contents

Acknowledgements

I owe fulsome thanks to my friends in the Primary Schools Research and Development Group for their permission to draw extensively on the research report: *Curriculum Responsibility and Teacher Expertise in the Primary School – Five Studies.*

I owe thanks, too, to Marcia Rosen and Pamela Cotton for deciphering my writing and typing the manuscript.

Philip H. Taylor
Birmingham, 1986

Author's Preface

'For assistant teachers there shall be special posts in respect of which allowances over and above the scale salary shall be granted for special responsibilities, special work of an advanced character, special academic qualifications or other circumstances.'

Burnham Committee Report, 1948

This book is more a contribution to a very necessary debate than a definitive statement about primary education today. In any event such a statement is hardly possible. Too much is unclear about the society in which we live, not least about the dependable features of its cultural and moral fabric.

In places, therefore, no more than a sketch or hint of something sensed has been possible; in others an effort has been made to clear the ground and open the road both back into the origins of modern primary schooling and on toward a possible future for it. One issue, however, holds the essay together, that concerning the expertise and responsibility of the primary school teacher; how these are constituted and what they may become. It is around the nature of these essential components of the teacher's role that the debate must take place if primary education is to improve. It is the aim of this work to raise the issues around which such a debate must take place.

Philip H. Taylor,
Birmingham,
January 1986

Part One

The Issue in Context

CHAPTER 1

The Changing Character of Primary Education

Introduction

This book addresses an issue that is central to the future of teaching and learning in the primary school, and one that should be of concern to all who have the interests of primary education at heart, no matter what their role and no matter what their status. It is an issue that if mishandled could introduce conflict and uncertainty into every primary school and lead to a sense of inadequacy on the part of many primary school teachers. As with other comparable issues, it is susceptible of oversimplification, dramatic, hyperbolic presentation and lends itself to polarized and impoverished debate with little room for the sensible development of a middle ground.

The essence of the issue is: how much a *curriculum generalist* and how much a *subject specialist* should the primary school teacher be? Put another way – what should be the expertise and responsibility of the primary school teacher? Behind the issue (in its extreme form rather than in its moderate version), lie competing theories of knowledge, of teaching and of learning. Associated with these competing theories of knowledge, teaching and learning are competing concepts of *literacy*, *numeracy* and *sociacy*. This last, *sociacy*, being a shorthand for that social and moral understanding which primary schools seek to develop throughout the years of primary education.

How these competing theories and concepts are handled as the issue is debated, may settle the nature of primary education well into the twenty-first century. Depending on how the issue is presented, the belief could become a received truth that subject based teaching in the primary school is a 'natural development', an 'organic' change in primary education when in fact it would represent a significant discontinuity in primary schooling. Conversely, it might come to be urged that the class teacher, the curriculum generalist, is the hinge on which all that is *good* in primary education turns. Such a view would be almost equally unsound. Both perspectives are too simplistic to be allowed to stand unchallenged.

As doubtful an argument is the one which attempts to demonstrate that any change in the present arrangements in primary schools would be a threat to the freedom that primary school teachers believe they exercise over what they teach and the power they wield in *their* classrooms. Both *more* freedom and *more* power to teachers might well be theirs under other working arrangements than generally exist at present.

Whatever the case, matters of 'freedom, 'power' and 'authority' cannot be ignored in the debate whether it is the freedom, power and authority assumed by those who work in primary schools or that exercised by those with responsibility for interpreting the interests of society, with its pressing political and economic concerns. Here no one person or agency will have the final word – not the Secretary of State, nor HMIs, nor educational theorists, nor local authorities, nor parents, nor the teachers themselves and their associations. Some will exercise more influence than others in promoting their point of view and seeking to see that it affects curriculum policy and practice in the schools.

In its milder form the issue was raised in the report of the 1978 HM Inspectorates' *Survey of Primary Education*[1], especially in Chapter 8: 'The Main Findings, Issues and Recommendations'. Under the sub-heading (iii) Class and Specialist Teaching, the report called for 'a fuller use of a teacher's particular strengths' and of 'expertise' in relation to 'specialist' teaching. It was also clearly envisaged that many teachers with posts of special responsibility should not only be *experts* in one or other curriculum area but also be responsible for the evaluation of the teaching of the curriculum area over which they have a responsibility throughout the school. However, the survey was ambivalent about how far the primary school teacher should be a curriculum generalist or a subject specialist. The advantage and disadvantages of both roles were rehearsed. The first, described as 'the traditional view', was thought to have 'important advantages' and should be retained. Even so the introduction of more specialist teaching in the primary school was by no means ruled out. It should not, however, be taken for granted that the question of the primary school teacher as curriculum *generalist* (class teacher) or a *subject specialist* has its origins solely, or even largely, in the pronouncements of Her Majesty's Inspectorate, though the Inspectorate has recently made the running. The issue may well have its roots elsewhere, most probably in the cultural conditions that have shaped much of modern society. It is after all these cultural conditions that have shaped what we believe primary education to be and have given to it qualities of *primariness* which we expect to find to some extent in all primary schools. It is the changing nature of *primariness* that we shall now examine, attempting as we do so to widen the grounds of the debate by giving to it an historical perspective.

The changing nature of primary education

There are two important sources for anyone interested in analysing the changing nature of *primariness* in primary education. One is from the way those responsible for primary education talk and write about it, especially in the metaphors they use[2]. The other is from an examination of the purpose that primary schools are encouraged to pursue. The first source reveals the general character and relevancy of primary education at a particular time: its predominant qualities. The second, its governing conditions: the aims that are held as valid for primary schooling.

Primariness, then and now

The root metaphor for primary education at the beginning of this century is to be found in its most precise form on the title page of the *Handbook of Suggestions for Teachers and Others Concerned in Elementary Education*[3], published in 1905 by the Board of Education. It is quite simply: 'The most important thing that is taught in the elementary school is the teacher himself.' This acutely teacher-centred metaphor is echoed throughout the *Handbook*. It is the teacher's role to impart knowledge, to dominate the educational stage and in every respect be *the* prime example; the child was cast as a passive learner and rote methods predominated, knowledge was conceived as 'building blocks' of information, the teacher as the master builder.

This view of primary education was not unrelated to the idea that children were 'ignorant' and needed through the ministering of the teacher to be brought to an educational state of grace. It was the teacher that opened the door to the kingdom of knowledge – or rather provided keys to it. The keys were the elements of literacy, numeracy and sociacy, especially good time-keeping and moral probity, together with some drawing and suitable craftwork. Music, mainly singing, also played a part as did physical training.

Teaching methods were in fact formal, even rigid, varying little from day to day. Discipline was strict and punishment physical, though fairly administered. Syllabuses were limited and strictly adhered to. Schools were highly organized, their function to provide a limited, largely cognitive education of a restricted kind using repetition and memorization as the basic tools of learning.

Within this limited framework, standards were good. The 3Rs were placed within the grasp of more and more children and external inspections kept everyone on their toes. Children were not thought of as 'creative' nor as entitled to an emotional life of their own, and they were most certainly not expected to question the teacher's knowledge. They were taught good manners, and respect for their elders and betters and to accept the social class into which they were born. They were not told why nor were they encouraged to accord meaning to their experience. Meaning was for others to determine. Others knew best.

Educationally, teachers presided over a limited territory. Many were poorly educated. Even so most believed that there was a *best* method for teaching reading, a *right* way to form one's letters, a *correct* way of speaking and a *precise* grammar to be employed in writing. Similarly with the teaching of arithmetic, there were *right* and *wrong* ways of setting out one's work. As for social and moral attributes, they had no doubts what these were: habits of industry, self control, perseverence in the face of difficulties, self-sacrifice, striving for the truth, a sense of duty, and respect for others.

It is not, therefore, surprising that teachers felt it right that teaching should be construed as a one-way transmission process made up of telling and learning, largely a process of recitation, copying and memorization.

From elementary to primary education

The *primariness* of the turn of the century was functionally robust. It worked very well within its limits and still has its advocates. But war, want and growing social and political complexity called for skills other, and beyond, those passively acquired rudimentary capabilities of reading, writing, arithemetic, together with a knowledge of the capes and bays around our coast and the names of the kings and queens of England. What was needed was a body of people who could *apply* their minds to a wide variety of unrehearsed situations. This ability requires the learner to grapple with problems, to apply principles in a variety of circumstances, to understand what he is doing and give meaning to his experience.[4] The last thing that was wanted was a passive response to the *right* answer or the correct method.

The Hadow Report of 1931, *Primary Education*[5], grasped this and captured it in a metaphor still frequently referred to and which informs the whole report:' . . . the curriculum is to be thought of in terms of activity and experience rather than of knowledge to be acquired and facts to be stored.' *Activity* was to become a key word, so was *interest*. With them came the need for a more relaxed atmosphere in the primary school classroom and the use of a wider range of teaching methods across a greater variety of content. There also developed a view of the child which allowed for the education of his emotions through art, drama and free writing. The child was not yet seen as creative but he was accorded more psychological space in the environment of schooling. Literacy and numeracy were beginning to expand beyond the 3Rs and sociacy beyond good time-keeping and good manners. However, the Scholarship Examination, later to become the 11+, kept much passive learning in place. Even so, by the outbreak of the Second World War, the nature of *primariness* had changed both in its theory and its practice.

It was a *primariness* that saw the now better educated teachers managing a more complex educational environment, holding a more sophisticated appreciation of the psychology of childhood, of how children learned and felt. The much expanded resources of books and materials on which they could draw, enabled them to go beyond the teaching of the 3Rs as tool subjects to the much more demanding teaching for understanding and meaning; to the creation of educational circumstances in which, more and more, children became self-confidently literate and numerate. This *primariness* paradoxically improved the quality of education that children received, and did so in circumstances which were pedagogically more various and supported by a richer range of resources – better educated teachers, a wider selection of textbooks and other educational materials – while at the same time removing from the teacher that pre-eminence of role that her predecessors had enjoyed. Teachers were now expected to take account of the interests of children and their need for emotional nourishment as well as to begin to accept, at least in part, that the growing child could legitimately give meaning to his own experience. Knowledge was no longer entirely the teachers' to dispense.

This move toward child centredness in primary education was to amplify in the thirty years following the Hadow Report, sustained partly by the influence of theories of child development and partly – and again paradoxically – by the teachers' need for increased professional autonomy; an autonomy achieved partly at least out of growing professional knowledge, especially the psychology of childhood through the application of theories of play and early learning, to primary education. Teaching was, at least in theory, no longer the simple, didactic process that it had been. Teachers were now required to take into account certain salient features of a child's development and vary their pedagogic approach accordingly. Teaching was becoming more 'scientific', less 'natural', and was edging toward claims to being based on professional knowledge.

After the Second World War, 'free activity', 'the play way' and 'readiness' were to become bywords in primary education and a persuasive rhetoric was developed to give them meaning, culminating in the root metaphor of the 1952 *Handbook of Suggestions*[6]: 'First the blade, and then the ear, then the full corn shall appear.' Primary education came to be conceived as cultivation: the creation of the right climate for the growth and development of the *whole child*. This horticultural metaphor was to permeate, and be the justification for, the pedagogic developments of the 1950s and 1960s. The primary school classroom was to become an altogether more colourful place with pictures and displays aimed to stimulate children's interests; with children's own work increasingly on show. Children moved about in such classrooms. No longer passive learners, they took a hand in their own intellectual, emotional and social growth. Children created their own art, wrote their own poetry, made their own music and developed their own literature; they wrote out of their own emotions and sensibilities. Learning by repetition was to disappear in many schools by the end of this period which was still constrained, at least at the upper end of the primary school, by the eleven plus examination.

Arithmetic was giving way to 'number work'. Reading and writing to 'language work'. Almost every area of activity in the primary school could find a *theory* – whether for free writing or art, mathematics or music. There was also strong theoretical support for local or environmental studies and for topic work.

Plowden and its impact

With the Plowden Report (1967)[7], child-centred primary education reached its most complete form. Its root metaphor, echoed in the title of the report, *Children and their Primary Schools,* was quite simply: 'The child is the centre of the educational stage,' a metaphor as positively emphatic in form as that which was the linchpin of the 1905 *Handbook of Suggestions for Teachers.*

Plowden dethroned the teacher as surely as the 1905 *Handbook* conferred on the teacher imperial status. Plowden cast the teacher as the producer-director of educational situations aimed at stimulating the child's interests and awakening his curiosity, and with a light touch steering the child in desirable directions. But it was the child who was to be the prime mover in his own learning. The impetus for this was to be as much self-motivation as teacher stimulation. Certainly the teacher was not expected to prescribe what was to be learned. Flexibility of pedagogic approach was to become an important weapon in the teacher's armoury, and 'openness' a keyword. Even so, children were expected to learn to read, write and calculate.

In making its recommendations, the Plowden Report drew on the physiology and psychology of childhood.[8] In this last, particularly on the work of the Swiss psychologist, Piaget, who had defined intellectual development as a matter of stages which could not be bypassed nor reached any sooner than the maturation of the child allowed.

The work of Piaget, at least in its naive form, led to a rash of studies, re-inforcing the idea that each stage in intellectual maturation had to be catered to and could not be hurried on. Teaching became, as a consequence, less formal and less structured: formal presentation of knowledge was considered less likely to give rise to meaningful learning; teachers were less concerned with achievement and more with the child's enjoyment of and satisfaction with learning. A prime aim of primary schools was 'to be a happy place'.[9]

Open-plan schools, pioneered in the immediate pre-Plowden period, with strong support – not only in the Plowden Report but also from the Schools Building Branch of the Department of Education and Science[10] – were built in increasing numbers and open-plan schooling saw many primary schools open classroom doors and spill their pupils into corridors and cloakrooms. The atmosphere of the school became to the outsider chaotic; a hub-bub of ceaseless activity with children working individually, in small groups and, very occasionally, as a whole class. Textbooks were increasingly replaced by structured teaching materials and class libraries, and the voice of children could be heard as frequently, if not more frequently, as that of the teacher. Children were chastised more for interrupting the work of other children than for failing to pay attention to their teachers.

Oxfordshire and Leicestershire were local authorities notable for pioneering this Plowden style of primary schooling, and for a short period British open primary education became internationally recognized and sought after. Schools in the Inner London Education Authority, illustrating variants of the 'open classrooms' were visited by American educators in hordes. Funds were even made available to 'export' open education to the United States.[11]

But 'open education' had its critics. The publication of a series of *Black Papers*[12] revealed just how deep was the rift between public understanding and the primariness of primary schooling in the late 1960s and 1970s. The charges of the Black Papers were that standards in the basic subjects had fallen precipitately, that many – if not most – primary schools were no longer clear what they were in business to achieve and most primary teachers had embraced an ill-digested philosophy of education.

Certainly some primary schools had lost their way and many teachers had become unsure what ends their teaching should serve. This state of affairs was brought about as much, if not more, by the abolition of the eleven plus which followed the spread in many local authorities of non-selective comprehensive secondary schooling as by the increasing child-centredness of primary education. The facts of the matter were that only a minority of primary schools were ever *pure* Plowden and even fewer were genuinely 'open'.[13] There was no revolution in primary education except perhaps in the rhetoric of primariness, but there were substantial changes.[14]

Post Plowden: The Great Debate

Hard on the heels of Plowden came the 'new' maths, primary science and 'oracy', the ability to talk and to listen, together with the many initiatives of the Schools Council. All of these made new demands on teachers; demands which in time would tend to push teachers toward teaching and away from children learning. In fact child-centredness in primary education which, according to the rhetoric of the teaching profession, was aimed at developing the child's full potential, was to come under pressure from another source. In 1976, at Ruskin College, Oxford, the then Prime Minister, James Callaghan, made a speech calling for a *Great Debate*[15] on 'education', the essentials of which were to determine what schools should be expected to achieve and to what degree they should serve the needs of the individual and to what extent the needs of society.

The debate, if such a stage managed series of meetings could be called, resulted in a *back-to-basics* movement and the demand for higher achievement in mathematics and language – especially in reading – in which standards were judged to be static, if not falling, though the data of the 1970 Survey of Reading Standards[16] on which this judgement was based were dubious. *Standards* became the watchword, reinforced by the Assessment of Performance Unit which was created by the Department of Education and Science to monitor standards in a wide range of curriculum areas and which failed to find an acceptable means for assessing standards, in social and moral education.[17] Monitoring, assessing and evaluation rapidly became part of the vocabulary of the managers of primary education. Primary schools felt the burden of criticism, and though what limited evidence there was suggested that primary school teachers had never neglected the basics, schools became less sure about the nature of the primariness that was to inform their work.

The Primary Survey

The publication in 1978 of the survey by HM Inspectors of Schools, *Primary Education in England,* was to bring little aid to those teachers committed to Plowden primariness and to invite what could be the beginning of a radical shift in the nature of primary education: an altogether altered primariness to guide the work of the schools. The foreword to the survey sets it out so:

> What emerges from the report is that teachers in primary schools work hard to make pupils well behaved, literate and numerate. They are concerned for individual children, and especially for those who find it difficult to learn. If the schools are considered as a whole, it is clear that children are introduced to a wide range of knowledge and skills.
>
> The efforts of children and teachers have produced encouraging results in the reading test for 11 year olds, where objective comparison can be made with the past; there is no comparable objective evidence of past standards in other parts of the curriculum. In some aspects of the work the results are sometimes disappointing. The reasons for this vary, and rarely stem from inattention and poor effort. In some cases the evidence clearly suggests that difficulty arises because individual teachers are trying to cover too much unaided. Some fairly modest readjustment of teachers' roles would allow those with special interests and gifts to use them more widely, as is shown in some classes where particularly successful work is done.

Clearly the praise for primary school teachers is muted, as is the criticism, and the suggested role revision is cautious. The language is judicious, stressing objectivity and evidence. This is true not only in the foreword but also throughout the report of the survey. Nowhere does an informing metaphor emerge, though in Chapter

8, 'The Main Findings, Issues, and Recommendations' the word 'work' frequently appears, especially so when classroom activities, the curriculum and the professional development of teachers is discussed. This gives the report a down-to-earth, matter-of-factness which contrasts markedly with the child-centred language of the Plowden Report. It is work-a-day in tone.

The low-key language of the survey is clearly deliberate. It is after all reporting *findings* not *results* of the deliberations of a committee, as was the case with Plowden. Even so, something can be discerned from these findings about the qualities of primariness that were found to be commendable.

In a systematic analysis of the report Dearden[18] found it to be 'unPlowden-like' in its emphasis on:

' . . . an "ordered and progressive curriculum" . . . '

' . . . the teaching of groups round the blackboard'

and

' . . . the unmistakable impression of thinking from secondary practices downward rather than, as with Plowden, thinking from infant school practices, upwards'.

He also noted that the idea of *specialist* teaching was commended as well as the fuller use of teachers' curricular strengths. Dearden, in his summing up points to the report's move towards a subject-centred view in contrast to the child-centred views of Plowden, going on to say: ' . . . this departure is not a return to fact-cramming or the rote learning of blocks of information, but an advocacy of stimulating intellectual development.' He does, however, criticize the emphasis on the learning of *skills* by the Inspectorate as the means for stimulating intellectual development as 'largely a misconception'.

Concentration on work *as subject matter,* on teachers' levels of knowledge and ability to organize programmes of work 'well suited to the capacities' of the children together with a view of the curriculum as 'the work of children' and the classroom as 'the general setting for work' lends more than incidental support to Dearden's view that one major recommendation of the report is to move primary school teachers toward a more subject-knowledge-centred view of the primariness that it is their role to realize. Another is that it is the aim of teachers' use of subject matter to realize through teaching the development of those capabilities that are seen to be crucial to the intellectual development of the child. Controlled, well-informed teaching rooted in explanation in addition to children learning by inquiry and discovery is considered to be a likely *best* method to achieve the desired qualities in primary schooling.

Plowden primariness has not been supplanted, though its frequently asserted excess is moderated. In fact a balance is struck in the report of the survey between teacher-centred knowledge and child-centredness in primary education. However, it is in the reinstatement of the role of subject matter in the work of the school and the emphasis on skills that the report lends support to a radical reappraisal of primary education and is a reversal of a trend that the past half-century and more had endorsed. The focus of this reappraisal is on how best teachers may manage a curriculum which has developed in purpose and structure far beyond that of the elementary school at the turn of the century and with the rhetoric of the Plowden Report almost two decades behind it. In all essentials it is a call for primary school teachers to accept a changed responsibility and altered expertise. It is to an examination of how the responsibility and expertise of the teacher has developed over time that the next chapter is devoted.

References and notes

1. DEPARTMENT OF EDUCATION AND SCIENCE (1973). *Primary Education in England: a Survey by H.M. Inspectors of Schools*. London: HMSO.
2. For example see, TAYLOR, P.H. (1982). 'Metaphor and meaning in the curriculum: on opening windows on the not yet seen,' *Journal of Curriculum Theorizing* 4, 1, 209-16. MUNBY, H. (in press). *Journal of Curriculum Studies*. LAKOFF, G. and JOHNSON, M. (1980). *Metaphors We Live By*. Chicago: Chicago University Press.
3. BOARD OF EDUCATION (1905). *Handbook of Suggestions for Teachers and Others Concerned in Elementary Education*. London: HMSO.
4. BEEBY, C.E. (1966). *The Quality of Education in Developing Countries*. Cambridge, Mass.: Harvard University Press. In this book Beeby charts the changing expectations of education over one hundred years in developing countries in terms of the demands made of pupils and quality of teachers. Much the same proposition is being put here.
5. CONSULTATIVE COMMITTEE OF THE BOARD OF EDUCATION (1931). *Hadow Report: The Primary School*. London: HMSO.
6. MINISTRY OF EDUCATION (1952). *Handbook of Suggestions for Teachers*. London: HMSO.
7. CENTRAL ADVISORY COUNCIL FOR EDUCATION (1967). *Plowden Report: Children and their Primary Schools*. London: HMSO.
8. This was the first time that an official report had in the body of its deliberations taken account of the sciences which underpin the concept of child development.
9. Despite the fact that the Committee under Lady Plowden contained arguably the most influential philosopher of post-war England, A.J. Ayer, the section on *The Aims of Primary Education* showed little or no philosophic insight. Of interest also is the ahistorical framing of the Report. Unlike most of its predecessors, the Report did not set primary education in an historical context.
10. The Schools Building Branch of the Department of Education and Science, rejuvenated after the Second World War, pioneered a new consortium approach to school building among local education authorities, winning a prize at the Triennial in Milan in 1960. See MACLURE, S. (1984). *Educational Development and School Building*. London: Longman.
11. The Ford Foundation of New York funded the publication of a series of teachers' guides edited by Maurice Kogan and published under such titles as *The Pupil's Day, The Head Teacher's Role* and *Recording Children's Progress*, all published by the Schools Council.
12. See COX, C. and DYSON, T. (Eds) (1975, 1977). *Black Paper*. London: Dent and Temple Smith and (1969). *Fight for Education*. London: Critical Quarterly Society.
13. The survey contained in BENNETT, S.N., *et al.* (1976). *Teaching Styles and Pupil Progress*. London: Open Books, is evidence of this.

14. There is ample evidence of this in RICHARDS, C. (Ed) (1982). *New Directions in Primary Education*. Lewes: Falmer Press.
15. The speech was made at Ruskin College, Oxford in 1976 and in printed form was entitled 'Towards a National Debate'.
16. A later study of reading standards undertaken by the National Foundation for Educational Research for the 1978 HMI Primary Survey, confirmed the continuing rise in standards since 1955.
17. The Assessment of Performance Unit was established by the Department of Education and Science in 1975. Monitoring has taken place in language, mathematics and science. For a critical appraisal see GIPPS, C. (1980). 'A critique of the A.P.U.' In: NUTTALL, D. (ed) 'Assessing Educational Achievement,' *Educational Analysis*, 4, 3, 57-68.
18. DEARDEN, R.F., see 'Balance and Coherence: some curricula principles in recent reports.' In: DEARDEN, R.F. (1984). *Theory and Practice in Education*. London: Routledge and Kegan Paul. Also see ROLAND, S. (in press) 'Where is Primary Education Going?' *Journal of Curriculum Studies*.

CHAPTER 2

Expertise and Responsibility in Perspective

Introduction

In the first chapter we saw how views about the nature of primary education, those salient qualities of primariness in primary schooling, have changed since the beginning of the century. In this chapter we shall examine the changing demands made on teachers of young children over the same period. Inevitably this will mean going over some of the same ground again but with a different end in view: that of seeking to understand the nature and conditions of a primary teacher's expertise and responsibility.

At the beginning of this century the term *primary* to refer to the early years of education had not been coined let alone officially adopted. It was not in general use until after the 1944 Education Act. Moreover, the habit of sending our children to school had not yet become established among the rural and urban poor. The nation was small by today's standards and, by today's standards, religious. More than half the population went regularly to church. Both private and public life were very different from now. Beliefs about children and human nature were, for the most part, untouched by the then *modern* science of psychology. But like today, the country was seeking a way out of an economic depression.

It was in relation to such a society and in a country of undoubted world standing that the shape of a twentieth century education for young children was being forged. Its manifesto is to be found in the *Revised Code of 1905*;[1] a manifesto which was to remain little altered for three decades until the *Hadow Report*[2] of 1931. Whatever alterations were made to the Revised Code were toward liberalizing the education of the young, even opening it to innovation and experiment and in dropping the annual inspection of schools begun under the notorious Payments by Results Act of 1870.[3]

At the heart of the *Code* or *Revised Code of Regulations for Public Elementary Schools,* as it became after 1905, was the primacy of the teacher. It was they, the teachers, asserted the Code, who:

> . . . though their opportunities are but brief can yet do much to lay the foundations of conduct. They can endeavour, by example and influence, aided by the sense of discipline that should pervade the school, to implant in the children habits of industry, self-control and courageous perseverence in the face of difficulties; they can teach them to reverance what is noble, to be ready for self-sacrifice, and to strive their utmost after purity and truth: they can foster a strong respect for duty, and that consideration and respect for others which must be the foundation of unselfishness and the true basis of good manners . . .

The responsibilities placed on the teachers were awesome; the rhetoric uncompromising and echoed not only in every subsequent publication of this Code but also in the *Handbook of Suggestions for the Consideration of Teachers and Others Concerned in the Work of the Public Elementary Schools.*[4] In every edition up to, and including that of 1927, it remained:

> . . . the high function of the teacher to prepare the child for the life of the good citizen, to create or foster the aptitude for work . . . and develop those features of character which are most readily influenced by school life such as loyalty to comrades, loyalty to institutions, unselfishness and an orderly and disciplined habit of mind.

Character training, if not all, loomed large.

At least this was the rhetoric. Parents and employers could, and did, demand the 3Rs, and teachers taught them with increasing skill as they became better educated. But the conflict of interests was there, as it is today, between the instrumental and ideal aims of education; between the rhetoric and the reality.

But it would be as mistaken to believe that rhetoric serves no purpose in education as to believe, as did the authors of the Black Papers that the rhetoric *is* the reality. In those areas of human affairs concerned with moral matters, with those endeavours to improve the human condition in other than material ways, in religion, politics and education, for example, rhetoric is both the language of persuasion and the language which sustains and directs effort. It is language replete with metaphor. It is the language of the manifesto, dangerous when taken too literally, invaluable as a guide to the criteria which should govern decision and choice, and stamp them as *good* and *right*: giving them social legitimacy.

Education for character

It was the case that the elementary school teacher was responsible for the development of valued qualities of character in the children in their care; for the cultivation of industry, discipline, self-control, perseverence, a sense of duty, orderliness, unselfishness, good manners, respect for truth and an awareness of the nature of nobility and of *noblesse oblige*. Everything they taught, it could be argued, served one or more of these ends. So could how they taught it, what they expected in the behaviour of the children whom they taught, and the way in which the school was organized and run. The education which they provided, which was more, much more, than the sum of what was taught, helped shape the identity of the children in their charge. At one and the same time it curbed the spontaneous desires of the child *and* set him standards by which to govern his behaviour both at work and at play. It also offered them an entry into the *best* of the life of the times.

In the intervening half-century much has changed but little altered. There is no longer an *official* manifesto for primary education in relation to which a rhetoric of justification can be developed to guide decision and choice, though there have been sources of rhetoric in official reports on primary education. The most notable of which were the Hadow and the Plowden Reports of 1931 and 1967[5], each of which, as has already been shown, sought to establish two principles: that primary education was not preparatory to secondary but an independent stage in education and should be centred on the child, his needs and interests.

The Hadow Report asked the question of primary schools:

Is their curriculum humane and realistic, unencumbered by the dead wood of formal tradition, quickened by enquiring and experiment, and inspired most not by attachment to conventional methodologies but by a vivid appreciation of the needs of the children themselves?

and turned for inspiration to the views about the education of the very young child arising from the newly developed sciences of child study and given intellectual respectability in the work of such scholars as Susan Isaacs[6] and C.W. Valentine.[7]

The rejection of a didactically taught curriculum of subjects in favour of a topic centred or thematic approach was also argued. The door to experiment in primary education was opened, though the 'free place' examination, later to become the 11+, together with the physical conditions of many primary schools, ensured that educational experiment would be severely constrained for another quarter of a century.

Changing responsibilities: Plowden and beyond

The Plowden Report confirmed many of the proposals of the Hadow Report and did so more surely drawing on thirty years of work in the psychology of childhood and more than a decade of innovation in the education of very young children. Teaching was to be child-centred. At the heart of the educational process, said the Report, 'lies the child'. The curriculum was to be thought of in 'broad terms' rather than as a collection of discrete subjects. Categories, such as language, environmental studies, mathematics, expressive arts and science were to be preferred to English, arithmetic, geography, art, music and so on.

It was, however, for the Plowden Report to spell out the responsibilities of the teacher in the child-centred education while confirming the need for every teacher to be a good moral example though doing so with much less rhetorical flourish than in early official publications.

It was on the need for both a greater knowledge of subject matter and a greater knowledge of how children learn that the Report focussed, speaking of the 'frightfully high' demands that a child-centred education would make of teachers:

> . . . teachers who have continually to exercise judgment, think on their feet, to keep in mind long and short term objectives. They have to select an environment which will encourage curiosity, focus attention on enquiries that will lead to useful discoveries, to collaborate with children, to lead from behind . . .

Despite the fact that the Plowden Report did not give rise to the hoped for revolution in primary education, it did help establish the view that by the latter part of the century the primary school teacher needed to be significantly more knowledgeable than his predecessor, especially in curricular matters. Understanding mathematics is an altogether different matter from knowing the processes of arithmetic, just as understanding language, as was to become evident in the Bullock Report, *A Language for Life,*[8] is altogether more demanding than knowing what comprehension exercises or composition topics to select and the criteria by which to mark them.

The view that there was a need for teachers to become more knowledgeable than their predecessors about how children learn and can be motivated was not as securely accepted as the view that teachers' knowledge of literacy and numeracy needed to become more sophisticated, partly because the curriculum development movement of the 1960s and early 1970s drew attention more to the contents of education than to its processes and partly because the theories of learning and its language remained remote from the realities of teaching except in the education of very young children. In this respect one can contrast the work of Entwistle[9] with that of Donaldson[10] on how young children think. The former, though an excellent introduction to educational psychology, does not address the questions to which most primary school teachers seek answers; the latter does.

The need to emphasize the teacher's responsibility for subject matter knowledge as functionally related to, if not wholly comprising, the content of primary education was taken up in the *H.M.I. Survey: Primary Education in England*[11] and reinforced in the *9-13 Middle School Survey*[12] on the basis of a statistically significant match between 'a greater degree of subject teaching and a better standard of work'. This was a stronger claim than was made in the 1978 *Primary School Survey* which asserted that poor teaching and an inadequate 'match' between the subject material content of their teaching and the age and abilities of children, especially the most able, was linked to the teacher's specialist subject knowledge.

In fact, when the second definition of subject teaching used in the *9-13 Middle School Survey* is employed, there is little or no difference between the standard of work achieved by teachers who did and those who did not study the subject they were teaching in initial training. The issue is thus one of subject *teaching* rather than subject *knowledge*. When the *9-13 Middle School Survey* suggests, as it does, that subject teaching could well be suitable in a number of subjects of the curriculum for many, if not all, those children most commonly to be found in the final year of primary education, it means subject *teaching* not subject *knowledge* though it speaks confusingly of subject teachers.

Generalist or specialist?

The Middle School Survey raises, in the most acute form so far, though only in relation to older primary school children, the question: Should the primary school teacher be a generalist, a class teacher in fact, or a specialist subject teacher? It is, as a matter of history, a question that has been raised in almost every official publication since the beginning of this century. As early as 1905 in *The Handbook of Suggestions for the Consideration of Teachers*,[13] the issue of teacher specialization was tentatively broached:

> In large schools the greater part of instruction in each class is generally assigned to one teacher, and this is the best arrangement if the teacher can treat each branch of the curriculum with success. If, however, the teachers are not proficient in all subjects alike, the work may be distributed so as to assign instructions to those members of staff who have special knowledge of them.

Even so, the *Handbook* came down in favour of class teaching stating: ' . . . the importance of preserving unity (class teaching) is the more profitable.'

By 1923, the revised *Handbook*[14] is less sure and argues for the 'judicious' use of teacher specialization as a means to curb the waste of talent in teaching. However, it must be emphasized that the *Handbook* was referring to the elementary school which catered at that time for children up to the age of twelve and in some areas, fourteen, and it is made clear in the *Handbook* that teacher specialization should be adopted 'especially in senior classes', though presumably specialized teaching is not excluded from use with younger children.

In practice a judicious use of teacher specialization has been common practice in primary schools for many years, especially in music and in physical education and games, and not unknown in handicraft for boys and needlework for girls, in French and sometimes in language work. Such teacher specialization accounted in large part for the distribution of posts of responsibility in schools noted in the 1978 *H.M.I. Survey*. Some 70 per cent of schools had post-holders for music and an almost similar number for physical education and games including swimming.

As must be evident, such teacher specialization occurs because of the shortage of specialist skills in a school rather than in order to curb the waste of talent in teaching. It was in a similar vein that the recommendation of the 1978 *H.M.I. Survey* on the fuller use of teachers' particular strengths was made. It was seen as a means for providing curricular support for the class teacher in subjects where he might be less than completely competent. Science and craft were noted as subjects in which there was a 'poor showing'. However, the further use of teachers' particular strengths was seen not as the complete solution to the problem but as 'a useful contribution' to its solution. Its complete solution was to be sought elsewhere; partly in the improved standing of teachers with posts of responsibility and the attitudes of other teachers toward them as well as through the in-service training of teachers with posts of responsibility, and partly in the use of specialist teaching in cases where a teacher is more than 'a little unsure' of a subject. Music was mentioned and science, 'at least for older children'.

Even where specialist teaching was employed the 1978 *H.M.I. Survey* was clear about the continuing need for a teacher to coordinate the programme of a class. Moreover, they warned of the dangers of the fragmentation of the work of the specialist teacher's own class. In all essentials class teaching with its traditional advantages was to remain intact despite the finding (mentioned earlier p.20) of the relationship between the subject matter content of teaching, the teacher's specialist subject knowledge and the quality of teaching.

Class teaching: its advantages

As has already been noted (p.20), since the beginning of the century, the advantages of class teaching in the education of young children have generally been preferred to those of specialist teaching. Why? The 1978 *H.M.I. Survey* makes these points in its favour:

the teacher can get to know the children well;
can get to know their strengths and weaknesses;
can readily adjust the daily programme to suit special circumstances;
can coordinate the curriculum, and
can reinforce the work done in one part of the curriculum with work done in another.

Earlier official writings argue that class teaching caters better for the interests of children, ensures that there is sympathetic concern for their well being, provides opportunities for personal guidance, ensures a balanced curriculum, caters for the development of such skills as handwriting and other non-subject specific capabilities as well as contributes to school unity.

However class teaching can mean something other than one teacher having responsibility for teaching one class for most if not all subjects, which is to be contrasted with specialist teaching where many teachers each teach a separate subject to the class.

Class teaching can also mean:

i)   teaching the whole class as one group,

ii)   teaching a class of children each individually, and with variants in between such as the class in small groups.

The educational benefits claimed for individualized teaching within a class in addition to those claimed for class teaching are many. Chief among them are that it can cater to the particular mode of learning most naturally adopted by a child – to his preferred learning style – and it can also allow for a greater and more active participation by the child in his own learning leading to a high level of satisfaction and enjoyment in learning. In addition, it has been claimed that individualized learning can lead to an educational environment which speaks of pride in accomplishment. It could, however, be argued that any formal good teaching should lead to the creation of just such an environment.

Whatever is the case, and it is not intended to argue it here, class teaching whatever its form, whether the teaching of individuals or of the class as a group, is expected to result in the creation of an environment for teaching thought most likely to result in desirable educational results. An environment consisting of the kind of interpersonal relationships through which the teacher can learn to know the children, their strengths and weaknesses, their interests and aversions, and how best to guide them through their difficulties, both educational and personal, as a result of which each child will feel understood and supported, and find satisfaction and enjoyment in learning; an environment which allows for the integration of knowledge, the deployment of a variety of teaching styles and in which a balanced curricular experience is provided.

The subject versus class teaching

There are costs as well as benefits to any decision or choice. This is as true in education as it is in other walks of human life. Some of the costs of class teaching have been noted (p.22). Here it is proposed to explore other aspects of the subject versus class teaching argument.

There are two themes which touch on the issue of subject teaching versus class teaching. Each has been rehearsed in almost every official publication on primary education since the turn of the century and echoed in the many discussions of recent years about the nature and purpose of primary education. They are:

What should children learn?
How should they learn it?

At the beginning of the century the answers were seen as obvious and largely uncontroversial. The curriculum for children up to the age of eleven was to be the 3Rs, reading, writing and arithmetic, together with the rudiments of history, geography, nature study, drawing, singing, handicraft and physical training. In addition, needlework and housecraft, hygiene and temperance would be found in many, if not all, schools. Most subjects were taught formally and didactically, by transmission from teacher to taught. Repetition, recitation and exercise were the predominant modes through which children were expected to learn; modes of learning which found justification in faculty psychology which argued that the faculties of reasoning and judgement were developed, like muscles, by exercise. The same was considered to be also true of faculties of tune and form. The acquisition of knowledge was seen as a prime objective of education. Whether or not children understood what they were able to repeat was not questioned.

As the educational system developed and became more differentiated with the senior class in the elementary school, central and grammar schools coming into being together with the pressure of the 11+ examination, and the free place or scholarship system coming into existence, some doubts were expressed about the formal subject-based curriculum for the youngest children in the elementary school and some uncertainty about when formal instruction in reading, writing and arithmetic should begin for older children. The *1923 Handbook of Suggestions*[15] put the matter this way:

> There can be no question that the use of reading and writing as instruments of thought should not be forced on children before they have acquired the raw material of observation and ideas which those instruments were designed to deal.

Attention was drawn to 'the needs and interests of the child himself' as a principle of curriculum decision. Even so, the subject as the unit of the curriculum was largely confirmed for children of eight, nine and ten years of age; even for some younger children.

It was not until the Hadow Report[16] of 1931, which was concerned with the education of children from seven to 11 years of age, that the subject basis of the curriculum for young children was challenged. One of its recommendations urged that: 'The traditional practice of dividing the matter of primary instruction into separate "subjects", taught in distinct lessons, should be reconsidered.'

The Report wrote vigorously on this issue, speaking of subjects as 'artificial', of knowledge as 'all of a piece', of the need for the curriculum to be 'vivid, realistic, a stream in motion not a stagnant pool', and 'to be thought of in terms of activity and experience rather than knowledge to be acquired and facts to be stored'.

Thus, one third into the twentieth century the role of subjects in the education of the primary school child was opened up. It was an issue closely related to the question of how far primary education should be preparatory to secondary education and how far it should be a phase of a child's education which was self-contained, with its own ends in view. If the last, how should its content be construed, if not in terms of subjects? To say, as did the Hadow Report, that it should be 'thought of in terms of activity and experience', is a recommendation about the way in which the curriculum should be handled but says little or nothing about its content. Inquiry and experiment inspired 'by a vivid appreciation of the needs and the children themselves' were to be the principles governing the selection of content which was to comprise 'fields of new and interesting experiences to be explored'. A final quotation from the Report, 'the education of children in primary schools must have a character of its own', tells why subjects were largely to be left out of account. Building blocks of the curriculum for the secondary school, but not the up and coming primary schools in which much the same creed was to apply to the education of children in the infant school (Hadow, 1933)[17]. It was to be: experiment and exploration in an 'instructive environment' rather than in a 'place of instruction'.

These sentiments did not mean that the subject basis of the primary school curriculum changed over night. It did, however, open the door to experiment, to the encouragement of theme teaching and topic work; in fact, to much that 'progressive' educationists and the new breed of child psychologists were advocating in the education of young children. To use a cliche, primary education was to become child rather than subject-centred.

Even so, the Hadow Report was forced, at least in part, to use a conventional terminology to indicate what it considered should be the content of the curriculum of the primary school. Language, especially oral expression and communication, was to be taught as was mathematics, in particular the familiar parts of arithemetic, the properties of spatial figures, area, volume and mensuration. Science, too, was to be taught, as the study of salient features of plant and animal life, outstanding physical facts and some astronomy. Aesthetic subjects had their place – handwork, drawing, painting, needlework, handwriting and music – some of which would develop manual skills as well as develop interests in aspects of 'the civilized life'. The beginnings of literature were not to be ignored nor were those of geography and history. Physical training and games were also to be included.

Intellectual disciplines and subject areas were to remain but within a changed concept of primariness. At the beginning of the century the aim of education for the young child was practical, to equip the mass of children with the rudiments of 'mental and moral equipment'.[18] By the time of the Hadow Report primariness was being seen as more about learning to learn, active participation in learning, experience of a wider range of subject matter and about understanding what one was taught rather than learning by rule and rote, delivered through a limited range of subject matter. With the Plowden Report came the right of the child to acquire intelligence out of his own curiosity and interests. But by then other factors were becoming salient.

Modernity and primary education

Accelerating social, economic and technological change has been a major characteristic of this century as of no other. Those concerned with primary education became increasingly aware of it as mid-century approached. 'Modern education', said the *1944 Handbook of Suggestions for Teachers*[19], 'must adapt itself to modern needs', and spoke of a more complex society, job changes, increased leisure and the democratic nature of our institutions as justification for a primariness in primary education which was not rooted in a knowledge of subject matter but sought to cultivate in every child an 'appetite for knowledge' and 'to develop his full potential'. Moreover, an increasing importance was to be attached to individual differences among children, not so much in terms of the knowledge they were able to acquire but in terms of their developed intelligence. The 11 plus selection procedure with its near ubiquitous IQ test was soon to come to dominate primariness in primary education but its justification was almost wholly based in the concept of individual differences in abilities and the function of the primary school to develop these, justified not only in terms of the natural development of the child but also in terms of the need modern society had for developed intelligence of every kind, especially mathematical, scientific and social.

It is concern with this stock of intelligence that is a salient feature of modernity. A modern society uses its educational system to ensure that the complex of systems which comprise it – economic, technological, legal, governmental and social – are able to draw on a stock of people who possess highly developed intellectual capabilities in an array of specialist fields; particularly in science and medicine, in mathematics, in the use of language for its employment in the practice of law and in government. The growing emphasis in primary education on increasingly high levels of literacy and numeracy, on intellectual understanding, learning for meaning and learning to learn, and on what has aptly been described as 'acquiring intelligence'[20] is directly related to increasingly modern society in which the primary school child was growing up. Not every child was expected to become a scientist, mathematician, lawyer, doctor or civil servant but every normal child was expected to be intelligent and eventually to take his place in a technical and literate society. What was coming to matter in the primariness of primary education was not so much what was taught but the quality of children's 'learning'.

The 1959 Handbook[21] was clear on this as it was on the methods that were to be employed to achieve it. Exploration and investigation were to be used to harness the child's curiosity, inventiveness and imagination to produce a high level of competence together with a lasting satisfaction in achievement. Certainly children were to be children. They were also expected to: ' . . . taste the satisfaction of achievement due to their own efforts', but not through subjects, that is until they became Upper Juniors. 'To adopt this classification,' said the Handbook, 'before children have any appreciation of its significance is to make school work artificial and remote from their experience of life.'

For Upper Juniors subjects were to emerge as language, mathematics, religious education, environmental studies, art and craft, music, physical education and games. Throughout the primary school the class teacher rather than the specialist was preferred. However, the *Handbook* went on to add:

> . . . yet the primary school is richer for any specialist knowledge or skill possessed by any of its teachers. Men and women who, for example, are naturalists, artists, musicians, historians or lovers of English

and the Head was counselled to:

> . . . make use of his staffs' special interests and knowledge . . . and to encourage members of his team to seek specialist help from each other when this is available.

The views of the 1959 Handbook were echoed in the Plowden Report. The intervening period – less than a decade – had seen widespread experiment in primary schooling in many local authorities, notably in Oxfordshire, the West Riding of Yorkshire, Leicestershire and in London. A freer and more open primary education was fast becoming the vogue. Much that earlier generations of educationists had argued about the nature of primary education had been progressively incorporated into official documents, and was being put into practice with varying degrees of success.

Three factors were responsible for the impetus to experiment. The abolition by local education authorities of the 11+ selection procedure, promoted from 1965 by central government's requirement for all authorities to put forward plans for a system of comprehensive secondary education; the growth in the child population which required an extensive primary school building programme which found support in the innovative architectural proposals of the newly created Schools Building Branch of the Ministry of Education;[22] and the growing public belief that education as an investment in the future mattered not only for the individual but also for the economic well-being of society.

Remarkably, an educational creed and the belief in the investment value of education at all levels came together in the 1960s to power one of the most remarkable phases in English education. It was to be a phase marked by vision and energy, and the thrust of a buoyant economy.

In primary education the vision is most clearly seen in the Plowden Report. Curricular freedom was its watchword; freedom from all but the interests and curiosities of the children it would serve to educate. Subject matter was to be thought of in broad terms – language, science, mathematics, environmental studies and expressive arts. But it was for the child to discover meaning in his curricular experience rather than be told the meaning he should give to it. Teaching was to be flexible in its use of subject matter. Individual and group work, the use of structured materials, especially in early language learning and in mathematics, and direct experience of the environment were to be encouraged. The didactic approach, based on whole class teaching, on chalk and talk, was to be firmly set aside as an appropriate mode for creating environments for learning with those qualities of vividness and intensity that would challenge children to learn and work out things for themselves. Children were expected to talk about what they did, discuss it with each other and the teacher, find out things for themselves, generally taking an active role in their own learning.

The Plowden Report[23] recognized that the teacher would require a whole range of new pedagogic skills and professional knowledge:

> . . . more knowledge both about subject matter and how children learn more in order to select an environment which will encourage curiosity, focus attention on enquiries that will lead to useful discoveries, to collaborate with children and to lead from behind.

The Report contrasted the Plowden teacher with the traditional teacher who 'could manage on little knowledge and use it over and over again'. Paradoxically, the Plowden teacher would need not only to know more subject matter but to know more about its structure; about the way in which it hung together as science, mathematics, history or geography, even though these last two were not seen as suitable subjects in their own right but only as 'dimensions in other work'. On the teacher's intellectual grasp of subject matter would depend the quality of children's learning not least in language, mathematics and science, that is if the children were to understand their nature. In fact many of the curriculum materials developed during the 1960s by the Nuffield Foundation[24] and the Schools Council[25] for primary schools were rooted in the assumption that to learn something properly was to know both how the knowledge entailed was obtained, at least in broad terms, and to understand its conceptual structure. That such could be learned by young children in some intellectually honest fashion had resulted from arguably the most influential educationist of the immediate postwar period, the cognitive psychologist, Jerome Bruner.[26]

Retrenchment

The Plowden vision was never to be implemented in more than a limited number of schools and even then only partially. The economic retrenchment of the 1970s and a 'back to basics' movement in the form of the Black Papers were to see to that. The Black Papers[27] argued for a return to the educational traditions of an earlier age, to formal teaching and measurable achievement, especially in reading, writing and such fundamentals of mathematics as tables and the four rules of numbers. Research findings based on studies of primary school classrooms reinforced the claims of the critics of Plowden-style teaching as did national studies of reading performance.

More than the Black Papers and the Bennett Studies[28] were to cast doubt on the achievements of primary schooling and the competence of primary school teachers. The whole educational system was to come under sharp public and political scrutiny; an economy in sharp recession needed scapegoats. Education was one. Seen no longer as an important investment in the Nation's People but increasingly as a cost to be borne by local and national government faced with the need to retrench, the efficiency of education was called into question. Issues of efficiency quickly led to questions of purpose and of whose interests were greatest, the children's or society's? The Great Debate, originated by a Labour Prime Minister (and mentioned earlier on p.9), started more than a critical assessment of schools and teachers which continues today. It presaged a change in the balance of power.[29] No longer were schools and teachers to be left to manage their own affairs, however respectful of suggestions from central government. Central government was intent on directly influencing what schools taught and monitoring their performance in terms of clearly specified objectives. Accountability was the watchword: value for money, the underling principle; the consequences, plummetting teacher morale and the reinforcement of the traditional subject basis of the primary school curriculum. Studying a subject in some depth as part of the education of primary school teachers was to become mandatory, further reinforcing the importance to be placed on a teacher's subject knowledge.[30]

The 1978 HMI Survey,[31] as we have seen (p.11), added its weight during this period, paradoxically, not so much out of a concern for the quality of the content of teaching in primary schools, though that was real, but in the belief that the abolition of the 11+ had left many primary schools not only without clear curriculum aims but also without a substantive curriculum content. The concern expressed by the Survey about the subject expertise available to primary school teachers relates to the assumption that teaching has to have a content the quality of which is directly, though not wholly related to standards of achievement. That this assumption has become the basis nationally not only for discussing the primary school curriculum but also for constructing it is now clear. In the words of the Senior Chief Inspector[32] addressing the Annual Conference of the National Association for Primary Education:

I believe that the primary curriculum will be discussed largely in terms of subjects, and that there will be broad agreement about which subjects make up the curriculum and what the objectives of each should be. It is on the basis of those objectives that agreement could then be reached about the standards that can be expected to be achieved by the broad mass of pupils at age 11.

Later in the same address the Senior Chief Inspector raises the issue of the use of 'specialist expertise' that exists among primary school teachers especially in relation to the teaching of science, mathematics and the use of the micro-computer. Designating some teachers as subject consultants is one solution but clearly, not the favoured one. The heart of the matter, the key question is: When and how should the change from general class-based to specialist-based teaching take place? The justification for such a change, say at the age of 9, is that it would challenge and stretch all children resulting in higher standards of achievement.

The issue, as must be already clear, is not new in substance. It has returned, however, with renewed force. The Cockcroft

Committee[33] found that there was a seven-year range of achievement in mathematics among 11-year-olds. The Assessment of Performance Units[34] studies of achievement in science in primary schools demonstrated that there is much to be desired in what is taught as science, the evidence of the HMI 9-13 Middle School Survey[35] of the relationship of subject teaching and standards of achievement (already referred to, p.20) and the HMI study of probationary teachers[36] in schools cast doubt on the competence of up to one quarter of them. Such empirical and judicial evidence cannot readily be ignored. It has at least to be placed in the context of primary schooling today.

If improvements in standards are to be achieved, two things are needed. First, to explore the way forward, whether through a subject consultancy system, by the use of curriculum coordinators, or by the development of some other role, or by the introduction of subject specialist teaching at a point in the primary school. Second, to examine the primariness of primary education for the last two decades of this century. The first will be the subject of the next chapter. The second of the final chapter.

References and notes

1. BOARD OF EDUCATION (1905). *Code of Regulations for Public Elementary Schools.* HMSO.
2. BOARD OF EDUCATION. CONSULTATIVE COMMITTEE (1931). *The Primary School: the Hadow Report.* London: HMSO.
3. The Elementary Education Act (1870) was introduced to the House of Commons by W.E. Forster. Its aim was to provide sufficient efficient and suitable elementary education for the labouring classes. The Act became notorious for its basis in inspection and payments by results.
4. BOARD OF EDUCATION (1905). *Handbook for Suggestions for the Consideration of Teachers and Others Concerned in the Work of the Public Elementary Schools.* London: HMSO.
5. CENTRAL ADVISORY COUNCIL FOR EDUCATION (ENGLAND) (1967). *Children and their Primary Schools. Volume 1 and 2: The Plowden Report.* London: HMSO.
6. Susan Isaacs' classic, *The Children We Teach*, first published in 1932 was being reprinted almost twenty years later.
7. C.W. Valentine's *Introduction to Experimental Psychology and its Relation to Education*, was published in 1916 and his influential *The Normal Child and some of his Abnormalities*, as recently as 1960.
8. DEPARTMENT OF EDUCATION AND SCIENCE (1975). *A Language for Life: the Bullock Report.* London: HMSO.

9. ENTWISTLE, N. (1980). *Styles of Learning and Teaching.* London: John Wiley.
10. DONALDSON, M. (1978). *Children' Minds.* London: Fontana. In this connection, also see, TIZARD, B. and HUGHES, M. (1984). *Young Children Learning.* London: Fontana.
11. *Op. cit.*
12. DEPARTMENT OF EDUCATION AND SCIENCE (1983). *9-13 Middle Schools: An Illustrative Survey.* London: HMSO.
13. *Op. cit.*
14. *The Handbook of Suggestion,* unlike the *Code* which was revised annually, was revised at infrequent intervals.
15. Again, it should be noted that the *Handbook* was concerned with elementary not primary education.
16. *Op. cit.*
17. BOARD OF EDUCATION (1933). *Report of the Consultative Committee on Infant and Nursery Schools.* London: HMSO.
18. See 1905 *Code of Regulations for Public Elementary Schools op. cit.*
19. MINISTRY OF EDUCATION (1944). *Handbook of Suggestions for Teachers.* London: HMSO.
20. The phrase was first used in the Minister's preface to the Newson Report. See CENTRAL ADVISORY COUNCIL FOR EDUCATION (ENGLAND) (1963). *Half Our Future.* London: HMSO.
21. MINISTRY OF EDUCATION (1959). *Handbook of Suggestions for Teachers.* London: HMSO.
22. See Chapter 1 page 8.
23. See Plowden Report, Volume One.
24. For example, see KERR, J. and ENGEL, E. (1982). *Should Science be Taught in the Primary School?* In: RICHARDS, C. (Ed) *New Directions in Primary Education.* Lewes: Falmer Press.
25. Very many Schools Council projects especially in science and mathematics aimed to introduce young children into the nature of the subject.
26. BRUNER, J. (1963). *The Process of Education.* New York: Vintage Books.
27. See COX, C. and DYSON, T. (1975, 1977). *Black Paper.* London: Dent and Temple Smith.
28. BENNETT, N. *et al.* (1976). *Teaching Styles and Pupil Progress.* London: Open Books.
29. For an analysis of power shifts in educational systems, see ARCHER, M.S. (1984). *Social Origins of Educational Systems.* London: Sage.
30. This is made clear in recent CATE guidelines related to the accreditation procedure now governing the new courses in teacher education. See DEPARTMENT OF EDUCATION AND SCIENCE (1984). Circular 3:84, *Teacher Training.* London: DES.
31. The Survey did so in its emphasis on its findings that the involvement in a programme of work led to improved basic skills.
32. The address entitled, *Current Issues in Primary Education* was delivered to the Annual Conference of NAPE.

33. DEPARTMENT OF EDUCATION AND SCIENCE (1982). *Mathematics Counts: the Cockcroft Report.* London: HMSO.
34. See, for example, DEPARTMENT OF EDUCATION AND SCIENCE, A.P.U. Reports (1981 and 1983). *Science in Schools: Age 11, Report nos. 1 and 2.* London: DES.
35. Especially, Chapter 8: Some Issues for Discussion.

Part Two

Some Evidence: How Teachers See Expertise and Responsibility

CHAPTER 3

Studies of Teachers' Views

Introduction

The studies that will be reported in this chapter arose from the suggestion in the 1978 HMI *Survey: Primary Education in England*[1] that one way of making fuller use of teachers' particular strengths would be to make their expertise more generally available by giving them responsibility for an aspect of the curriculum. They were carried out by a voluntary group of teachers and others concerned with primary education, and are abridged.[2]

At the heart of the studies was the concern to give those working in primary schools a voice: an opportunity to say what they thought constituted expertise and responsibility. The opportunity was also taken of testing the suggestions of the HMI *Survey* against the experience of practising teachers.

The methods employed were varied – group discussion, interviews, diaries, free accounts and questionnaires, both open-ended and closed. It was the last, the questionnaires, that gave the broadest sweep of opinion, the others gave colour and character to the findings. It will be for the reader to decide what reliance to place on the evidence presented. All data is fallible. But without data it is impossible to build up an adequate picture of a context that is not partial. The context which it is aimed to present here is that of the notion of expertise and responsibility, together with contingent issues that are current in primary schools today. We begin with the interviews.

The interviews: talking to teachers

'I might say I didn't ask for the post' –
Teacher with a Post of Responsibility

' . . . when I do look at the people who do have posts of responsibility I can't see that they do much more than I do' –
Teacher without a Post of Responsibility

Introduction

Why interview? Interviews possess a direct reality to which other instruments of social research cannot lay claim. Interviews are immediate and personal, and can be probing.

It was for this reason that they were undertaken. There could have been more of them and they could have been longer, but available resources meant that a choice had to be made between a small number of long interviews or a larger number of short interviews. It was made in favour of the latter. This is a report of twenty-two short, well-focussed interviews that follow.

The Interview Schedule☆

The questions contained in the first part of the Interview Schedule aimed to reveal how the system of posts of responsibility worked in the six schools of the twenty-two teachers interviewed. Additional questions explored how clearly those responsibilities were laid out, who influenced their style of operation, what kinds of influence the post-holders exerted and whether the system could be improved.

A second set of questions turned on the term 'expert' – especially in relation to responsibilities for curriculum areas. Other questions invited alternative words or phrases to that of 'expert' and sought reactions to the value of the *idea* of an 'expert' both in theory and in practice in the primary school.

No attempt to randomize the sample was made but fifteen of the

---

☆   See Appendix 1 for a copy of the Interview Schedule.

teachers interviewed held posts of responsibility and seven did not. The posts were for more than one area in half the cases, with mathematics being mentioned six times, language three, art two and all other only once. These other posts included religious education, music, physical education, dance and drama, environmental studies and science.

Table 1: The interview sample

Type of School	Interviewees
1 x Infant school (170 pupils)	4 teachers with posts of responsibility
4 x Infant/junior schools (290-610 pupils)	8 teachers with, and 7 teachers without, posts of responsibility
1 x Junior school (220 pupils)	3 teachers with posts of responsibility

The interviewees did not see the Interview Schedule beforehand – and while they were made aware of the research and its objectives they had no knowledge of the questions to be asked. The responses were therefore immediate and spontaneous, with little or no time available for reflection. The interviews were taped and deliberately brief, lasting from 20-30 minutes. Thus it was not often possible to pursue questions beyond a certain point. Although the schedule was semi-structured, the same basic questions were asked with follow-up queries if the responses seemed to lead in a different, but pertinent direction. For example, at the end of answering the second set of questions, it very soon emerged that teachers hardly ever visited or had knowledge of other schools – a fact which they regretted. As the interviewer considered this to be a useful issue to explore, a question to this effect was inserted in subsequent interviews.

Teachers with posts of responsibility

As was mentioned earlier, mathematics, language, reading, English, music, physical education all figured largely in the areas of the curriculum for which the teachers were responsible. Less frequently mentioned were dance, drama, religious education, art and craft. Most teachers were responsible for more than one area of the curriculum: 'Dance, gym, drama, environmental studies, science', said one teacher. Another stated: 'Library, language and reading'. However, there were degrees of specialization with a teacher being responsible for only one area of the curriculum. This was especially so in mathematics, language and music.

Some teachers were not responsible for a specific curriculum area but had responsibility for curriculum development in general or, as one put it: 'I am the co-ordinator of effort and activity throughout the Infant department and I liaise with other departments and the nursery', adding, as an afterthought: 'and with parents.'

One teacher was responsible for the school camp, another for 'display' and one had the combined responsibility for religious education and plants in and around the school.

Conditions of appointment

Few of the teachers interviews applied for their posts of responsibility. Most were *given* the post. As one interviewee put it disarmingly: 'I might say I didn't ask for the post.' Similarly, few were provided with a job description stating the scope of their responsibility, though two teachers could not recall whether or not they had been given a job description. Another said: 'If there is a job description, I haven't seen it.' Several teachers had been asked to write their own job descriptions, and one said: 'There wasn't a job description until I was asked to do one.' In the few cases where a job description existed, it either expected too much or was unrelated to the responsibilities which were being discharged. As one teacher retorted: 'Originally yes (it was accurate), but it doesn't describe what I do now.'

It is clear from the teachers' replies that neither the circumstances nor the conditions of appointment are in any way standard. There is, to say the least, a fair degree of ambiguity surrounding the scope of posts of responsibility – an ambiguity which some teachers are taking steps to moderate, though others – it must be said – continue to experience uncertainty about the nature of their responsibilities.

Advice: given or taken?

Teachers with a post of responsibility for an area of the primary school curriculum can reasonably expect to be a source of advice and most of the teachers interviewed accepted that this was so. Most stressed, however, the delicacy with which such advice should be given – many emphasizing the highly informal nature of their relations with their colleagues:

'Over coffee', said one.
'By example',
'In a mutual give and take',
'Only if they want help',
'It must be personal',
'When things come up'.

All of which serve to underline the circumspect character of the interactions between teachers with responsibility and other teachers in the school.

It was the general view that this informal system worked well leading at times to more formal discussions and meetings. It was also the case that staff meetings were frequently used as the occasion when teachers with responsibility for a curriculum area could pass on advice. One or two teachers operated more directly giving demonstration lessons or direct recommendations about using a mathematics or a reading scheme, but they were in a minority and the circumstances may well have arisen out of earlier informal contacts.

Generally, however, the ethos which teachers with posts of responsibility sought to preserve was that of mutuality, of collegiality and professional common interest and they would not venture advice unless it was requested, though one or two teachers added ruefully: 'Usually I'm asked when there is a problem.'

Despite the very low profile maintained by teachers with posts of responsibility and the fact that they must take up a very recessive role, they – along with their colleagues without posts of responsibility – believe the system works and is maybe the only system that could work, especially in small schools. They do, however, admit that there can be hiccups from time to time; that things may get done only slowly and sometimes not at all. Even so there is little evidence that they would seek to restructure the system along more formal lines, although there are some indications to suggest that improvements in this area are needed:

> I think we need to formalize the Language policy (of taking advice) to a large extent.

> I think in this particular area (art and craft), yes. I think if it were maths or English it would be slightly different.

> This is usually done informally and can also be raised at meetings. It certainly is a matter for concern.

With here some doubt expressed:

> I think the procedures (as above) are satisfactory, yes, on the whole.

and

> I think initially to break the ground – but no, it needs a lot more than this.

adding:

> This introducing a new scheme of Maths – which, when the money's available, is what we'll be doing. I think we'll need staff meetings – group meetings with the other departments of the school and also a bit of in-service work with people to come in and introduce the scheme and back up from them.

Whose is the influence?

It was in part the purpose of the interview to explore by whom and by what teachers with posts of responsibility were influenced and to what extent. From such evidence the degrees of freedom available to such teachers might become clear.

The head emerged as the most influential and LEA advisors as the least:

> Not really.
>
> Little help.
>
> I wouldn't say so.
>
> They offer nothing specific.

were the sort of comments made about LEA advisors, though there was the occasional redressing remark: 'I got a lot of guidance from them', from a teacher responsible for introducing a new mathematics scheme. Head teachers were seen as distinctly more potent influences:

> Head decides and we pass it on.
>
> Nothing gets done unless it's discussed with the head.
>
> One of my jobs is to help organize the kind of school he sees.

and

> I work within the head's guidelines.
>
> The head has the final say.

Some teachers find themselves less circumscribed by the heads than this:

> The head usually supports me.
>
> I'm given a certain amount of freedom.
>
> The head leaves a lot to me.

and

> A lot, I think.

The feeling conveyed even by those teachers who feel most free to exercise their responsibility in their own way is that it is the head's authority that is final.

Several teachers speak of 'working together', of the readiness of the head to be supportive and enabling, to encourage and to exchange views about a problem in an open and helpful way. It is by no means the case that heads are always seen as autocratic. They are, however, seen in the main as a dominant force in the school.

Other sources of influence such as teachers' guides, books and reports are much less potent than that of the head but more so than LEA advisors. They are described as 'helpful', 'useful' and 'a good resource'. It is, however, in-service courses that prompt the most positive comments:

> A great help.

> Oh, yes, very good.

> Definitely. Yes.

and

> Useful, in the main.

Some teachers regretted that they could not secure release to attend more courses and others that there was 'too little time'. Several teachers considered that some courses lacked relevance and showed little awareness of the issues facing the teacher.

The biter bit!

Just what influence do teachers with posts of responsibility believe they have? Obviously less than that of the head but more or less than other sources of influence? Some said yes, others no.

> I wouldn't say 'influence', said one teacher.

> People tend to ask me.

Others were less diffident:

Yes I think I have considerable influence.

Yes. It's a small school.

I hope so – with my enthusiasm.

Yes, I think I am in my own area.

Yes, I would say so.

But just as many doubted their influence and some whether influence was at all an appropriate term:

It's very difficult to say.

I wouldn't say so.

No, unless there is a problem.

I wouldn't try to, to be quite honest.

I wouldn't say 'influence', I would say advise people.

Hardly, but I'm always available.

Some difference of view does then exist among teachers with posts of responsibility concerning the influence they exercise, and it may be the case that in the informal system of the primary school, 'influence' smacks too much of power-coercive relationships which are foreign to the mutuality of informal systems and do not represent the reality of how things get done in primary schools. As will be seen in the next section, hard terms to describe roles and relationships tend to be rejected as legitimate means of describing the state of affairs as experienced by primary school teachers.

Expert or not?

'Is the term "teacher expert" appropriate for people with posts of special responsibility for a curriculum area?' was the question posed. The answers came in several sizes:

Off putting.

No, puts too much onus on the individual.

I couldn't possibly be an expert.

No, I don't actually.

Expert implies you keep to your little field.

No, to be honest I don't.

and

Well let me put it like this. I'm not really a Mathematics expert. I do Maths because I enjoy it. I'm more Maths minded than Art and Craft-minded, for instance, and I think an adviser would be a more appropriate term because I'm not an expert. I got Maths O-level but that's just about it . . . I've done it because I wanted to – I'm motivated in that area but I'm not an expert.

This notion that to be referred to as an *expert* requires that one possess formal qualifications runs through several of the responses as a reason for rejecting the term. As with the teacher quoted above, many teachers have taken on responsibility for a subject area because they enjoy the subject and 'have a natural interest in it'. Or, as one teacher replied: 'You need people who lean a little more toward one subject rather than another.' 'Adviser', 'consultant', 'inspirator', even 'gentle innovator' and 'coordinator' were preferred to *expert* as descriptions for teachers with posts of responsibility for a curriculum area, though a small minority of teachers were happy to embrace the term *expert*:

I like the term.

Yes, exactly so.

Good idea.

at least one of whom was clearly ambitious for preferment and promotion. If in general teachers with posts of responsibility rejected the notion of the expert, they most readily agreed that teacher expertise in curriculum areas was desirable, especially in the 'basic subjects' of language and mathematics, though most subject areas were mentioned. This quotation gives the flavour of the generally held view:

Yes, it is desirable. The background knowledge that everyone doesn't have – I find it useful to have someone to say to 'Look, I want to know this that or the other', and they can either answer me there and then or they can refer me to some sort of book or article . . . In the primary school . . . which curriculum areas? I'd say the academic subjects for reference – Maths and Reading, and Art and Craft subjects for help with presentation, and Music of course.

The availablity of expertise in curriculum and related areas is clearly seen as desirable. No one doubted this. It is how it should be made available that creates uncertainties. Undoubtedly the notion of the *teacher expert* is held at arm's length by most teachers. It does not represent their perceived capabilities as teachers with posts of responsibility, nor match the qualities of informality and recessiveness which most teachers with posts of responsibility would most readily embrace. It threatens to be authoritative which many teachers feel they could not lay claim to nor if they could, would wish to.

Improvement

Expertise is particularly susceptible of improvement, if not infinitely so. The teachers interviewed accepted this. They accepted the need to keep up-to-date; the need for in-service courses, especially those related to the realities of the classroom and the value of debate and discussion and of meetings, as means to improving their professional expertise and that of their colleagues. Some strongly expressed the need for and value of visiting other schools which they felt was difficult to do because of their commitment to class teaching.

Lack of time and incentives were seen as constraints to the improvement of teacher expertise. Promotion was seen as a major incentive – a problematic one in the present climate. Time is needed not only to improve expertise but also to pass it on. It is the dilemma of the primary school teacher to be required to teach a class and do it well, and be called upon to improve his expertise and have little time and scope in which to do so.

As much of a constraint on the improvement of their expertise, experienced by at least a minority of teachers was 'the aura of the head', and the head's control of information and opportunity. Some teachers expressed the view that if the school worked as a team then the readiness to improve would be enhanced.

But time is seen as critical to the improvement of expertise: witness the following:

> . . . one of the things is to give him time – that's always appreciated. Time to visit other classrooms – time to attend courses and meetings – I'm given *that* time, but I'm *not* given time to visit other classrooms.

Improvement in expertise is generally seen as entirely desirable, actively being sought but constrained not least by time and circumstances, and very much up to the initiative of the individual teacher. There was, however, a view representing a less *laissez-faire* perspective: 'I would like to see induction courses for all teachers given a scale 2 post.' Presumably such courses could only be mounted against a systematic analysis of the nature of the responsibility which post-holders were to discharge, its content and purpose. This more deliberate, formal approach, if it were to be more than ritualistic, poses many problems – one of which has emerged frequently from the teachers' expressed views – that teachers with scaled posts feel they belong to the informal system and believe this to be right.

Teachers without posts of responsibility

The seven

The seven teachers without posts of responsbility, with two exceptions, thought that the system of awarding posts of responsibility generally worked well enough. It was, in their view, sound in principle and in practice:

It makes things work smoothly.

Does ensure that various areas are covered.

Yes, no problem.

The system was seen by them as a means for relating teaching and administration. The exceptions were:

> I don't know really. I think everybody sees themselves as a 'class teacher' plus and sticks to the 'class teacher', because that takes up most of their time.

and

> Not very well, when I do look at the people who *do* have responsibility, I can't see that they do very much more than I do.

Views which will find later echoes and may resonate with some of the uncertainties expressed by some teachers with posts of responsibility.

Improving the system. Is it possible?

Several of the teachers without posts of responsibility considered that in-service courses would help in improving the quality of the system of posts of responsibility, especially training courses for post-holders. Others were uncertain:

> It's not a very clearly defined thing. There aren't any set rules.

> It seems silly to have someone responsible for an area.

The general impression was that improvement was possible but they were not sure how to bring it about.

Influence?

One teacher declared:

> I think it gives a lead to the other teachers within the school – as a sort of guide – to set down lines for you to follow, obviously if you

need it, and I think it works very well. If you have a specific problem in any of those areas, you can go and see the person with the scale post and they will help you.

But others expressed doubts about the influence exercised by teachers with posts of responsibility:

Not to any extent – or to the extent I think they should.

Not particularly so.

I think they should and I don't think they do.

Some teachers' replies accepted implicitly that teachers with posts of responsibility do exercise influence and valued qualities associated with it:

Help is given if asked for.

The personal touch is valuable.

Informally, yes.

'Expert' or not?

Teachers without posts of responsibility were less divided than teachers with posts of responsibility over the use of the term 'expert' to describe teachers with posts of responsibility. On the positive side:

Quite a good idea.

Useful.

Valuable.

Don't object to it.

were the generally favourable phrases used. On the negative side there were few comments, of which the following is the strongest:

I baulk at it. Almost everyone here is more knowledgeable than me. I really don't like the idea. It takes away autonomy in the classroom. In practical terms it's a dangerous thing to think you know all about it.

This from a teacher with little experience.

Improvement of expertise?

Could this be achieved and should it be attempted for all teachers in the primary school? 'Yes' was the virtually unanimous answer. But how?

Yes, contact with other schools.

Yes, but it's up to the individual.

By liaison between staff.

Yes, by revision of courses and by reading.

Courses, meetings, exchange of ideas and contact with other teachers were seen as means to the improvement of the expertise of teachers in the primary school. More pointedly:

I think some of these teachers (with posts of responsibility) should be sent on courses – and actually made to do something in their own subject.

and more generally it was felt that all teachers would benefit from refresher courses after a period of teaching.

Some reflections

From the rich fabric of the interviews there is much that can be gleaned. Some evidence, if that is what it is, points one way, some another. It is for the reader to follow the way it takes him or her. All that will be attempted here is not by way of conclusion but by way of deliberation on the findings of the interviews, some of which may be supported elsewhere and some not. Whichever is the case, it will focus on a human situation that is complex, composed of multiple realities and dependent as much on the nuances of relationships as on formal rules. As must be clear, this is true of that aspect of the primary school that has been the object of these interviews – the post of responsibility – and should not surprise us.

The profile of posts of responsibility is by no means clear. Most of those who hold such posts, though not all, claim the *informal system* as their locus of operation and all own that there is ambiguity, even woolliness, about their posts, though the few that see matters otherwise admit to a need for clarification and perceive it as a matter of concern – a view shared in large measure by their non-post-holding colleagues.

'Expert' is not a term most post-holders have any great wish to embrace. 'Adviser', yes, but nothing that would sharply distinguish them from their colleagues. Whether this is because, despite holding a post of responsibility they remain very like their colleagues, essentially class teachers or because being an expert in an area of teaching is altogether too problematic to lay claim to, is difficult to say. Their non-post-holding colleagues in general would not object to their laying claim to the distinctions which the term 'expert' implies, at least not to a greater extent than they themselves would.

But most post-holders would not seem to be free agents. With some exceptions, they seem to be the instruments of the head: to do his bidding, to realize his vision. Theirs is not to be responsible in any but a limited sense. It is to be constrained by the authority structure of the school in which they work. It is also to be constrained by the time they can give to the discharge of their responsibilities and the development of their grasp of the area for which they are responsible.

Post-holders or not, all the teachers interviewed accepted that expertise was their stock in trade and could be improved. Their notions of *how* were unsurprising and their readiness undoubted. Courses, meetings, an exchange of ideas with their colleagues, teachers' guides and other literature, with here and there the LEA advisor, were all potential sources of improvement in expertise – though, as has been said – there was simply not enough time to exploit them.

How best to resolve the evident uncertainties surrounding posts of responsibility *and* secure an improvement in the expertise of all primary school teachers as well as make that expertise more readily available at one and the same time is not easy to see. One way may be to take the 'naturally' occurring situation of collegial, informal, mutual interdependence among primary school teachers as the taken-for-granted-way of doing things and seek to make it work as well as possible with all teachers – whether post-holders or not – playing their part. Another is to make formal the informal; systematize it and develop governing criteria and monitor the extent to which the formal system meets the criteria.

An altogether more appealing way may be to run a 'mixed economy' requiring the more critical responsibilities for, say, post-Cockcroft[3] developments in mathematics teaching, to be accountable in formal and visible ways not dependent on 'goodwill', at least not more than is reasonable, and for these to be monitored.

For the rest, support for the informal system, sensitive and responsive to need, quietly providing help and encouragement where needed and when asked for, and drawing on expertise wherever it is to be found. Whichever approach is adopted, any of these or others, one thing is clear from the interviews: the way forward is neither plain to be seen nor is it likely to be simple to operate. The evidence which follows from some sixty heads and more than four hundred and fifty teachers may help to throw more light on the issues surrounding responsibility and expertise in the primary school.

The questionnaires

> A good example is better than a lot of theory – Head teacher

> I have developed the job as much as I wanted, but the base was "woolly" – Teacher with a Post of Responsibility

Introduction

In initially formulating the studies of which the questionnaire were part, a list of critical questions to be completed by teachers and heads grew. The questions were:

Who is the teacher 'expert'?

In what are they 'expert'?

For what are they responsible?

What are their backgrounds?

How do they see their role?

Do they have training requirements?

If so, what are they?

What, ideally, do they think they should do?

What do they do?

With whom do they make contact?

Over what?

How are they seen by their colleagues?

As the implication of each question was teased out in an attempt to ask it concretely and unambiguously, subsidiary questions presented themselves. In fact many more questions arose than could reasonably be asked, and in the end the questionnaires as completed represent a compromise; one which it is hoped will be seen to have produced a valid insight into the views of teachers and head teachers.

Heads respond

The questionnaire*

The main purpose of the questionnaire was to discover:

1.   The opinions of head teachers about the use of scale posts of responsibility in their schools.
2.   The amount of time teachers with such posts spent in discharging their responsibilities.

---

*   Details of both the heads' and teachers' questionnaires will be found in Appendices 2 and 3.

3. The criteria the heads would employ in appointing scale post-holders.
4. The ways in which heads might improve the standing of such teachers – a matter that was raised in the 1978, Primary Survey 'Primary Education in England : A Survey by H.M. Inspectors of Schools'.
5. The need for and the nature of the training of teachers with scale posts.
6. To whom such teachers should be responsible and how the exercise of their responsibilities should be monitored.
7. The heads' views on the present practices of appointing post-holders.

and finally,

8. Their reactions to suggestions in the Primary Survey that one way of making fuller use of teachers' particular strengths would be to make their expertise more generally available by giving them responsibility for an aspect of the curriculum.

In this connection the heads were asked whether teachers other than scale post-holders were given responsibility for areas of work, and if they were, for what they were responsible.

As one can see in Appendix 2 the questionnaire was very open. A matter, in the main, of a broad question with from four to twelve lines for the responses of the head, plus a page for any general comments that the head wished to make at the end of the questionnaire. It was hoped that by using this structure for the questionnaire a wide spectrum of freely expressed views would emerge.

The findings

Sixty-five head teachers completed the questionnaire very fully, and most provided detailed information about their practices and attitudes with respect to posts of responsibility. They also commented on the idea of the wider use of teacher expertise in the primary school, on the qualities needed in a post-holder, on improving the status of post-holders and on monitoring their work –

as the questionnaire required.

We propose here to deal with the broad findings, but before we do, a word about the head teachers who responded. More than half had been heads in their schools for six years or more and twenty-eight had held previous headships. The greatest majority had been trained as teachers in colleges. Very few held first or higher degrees. One was an acting head.

Allocation of scale posts

In all of the schools, scale posts were to be found. Most – around 50 per cent – were allocated for teaching, curriculum and resource responsibilities. These allocated posts covered responsibility for such things as language work, games, music and the library. The remaining 50 per cent of posts were allocated for welfare, liaison with other schools and administrative and organizational responsibilities. Responsibility for coordination, safety, first aid and specific groups of children made up only a very small proportion of posts. The posts allocated to teaching and curriculum responsibility (and more than one such post was allocated to these areas in many of the schools) were mainly to mathematics and language and reading skills, with a substantial number of posts allocated to art and crafts, science and music. Fewer posts were allocated to physical education and games, environmental studies and topic work and history, geography and social studies and fewest to religious education.

Within the general area of teaching and curriculum responsibilities most emphasis was placed on preparing schemes of work, managing resources and advising on teaching methods and least on advising on methods of assessments. To be fair, though, considerable emphasis *was* placed on assessments of mathematics and language work while there was little emphasis on assessment in other curriculum areas.

The heads expected most post-holders – around 60 per cent – to spend about a quarter of their time in school on their duties, though in some instances a post-holder was expected to spend all his time in school on them.

Responsibilities of 'other' teachers

Teachers other than those with scale posts are given responsibilities. Some for music, others for games or science or needlework. Some for health education or religious education, others for drama or remedial work, out of school visits and for audiovisual aids. Others have organizing or pastoral responsibility. Running the library or the lower school or a club may be an area of responsibility for other teachers, though in four schools all teachers had scale posts of responsibility.

The functions of these 'other' teachers were difficult to discern from the head teachers' responses. It was as if the label 'responsibility for science' was sufficient indication of the practical nature of the responsibility and was frequently the only indication given.

Qualities of office

The qualities which heads considered desirable in a potential post-holder in the area of curriculum and teaching were many and varied, and around these qualities heads said they would develop criteria for the selection of teachers to hold these posts. Tact, enthusiasm, wide and successful teaching experience, awareness, initiative, leadership abilities, concern for children, proven competence in a subject area, a modestly self-critical stance, empathy with the aims and ethos of the school, interest in change, verve, confidence and ambition were but a few of the qualities heads thought desirable. Others were:

In-depth knowledge of a curriculum area.
Interested in being up-to-date.
Able to arouse enthusiasm in colleagues.
Good qualifications.

and

Able to accept responsibility.
Willing to give of his own time.
Vision.

In fact heads gave between them more than one hundred and fifty characteristics that might be sought for in a post-holder. Not all qualities were wanted by every head nor in every school. One head cautioned, 'There is no room for strong dissention in a small group'. Some heads looked for the driving innovator. Others for the congenial facilitator.

Each school (or each head) sought a different blend of personal, professional and social qualities and skills. They all, as you would expect, gave prominence to professional qualities and experience, to knowledge of a subject area and to qualifications. They all also emphasized those interpersonal skills which make for sensitivity to others and the ability to secure the confidence and respect of colleagues. Among the professional qualities emphasized, in addition to the skills of teaching, were a sound philosophy of education which made for empathy with the aims of the school. Skills in planning schemes of work, in organizing resources and in demonstrating good teaching practices were also looked for.

Enhancing teachers with scale posts

'The status of teachers with posts of responsibility needs enhancing.' So said the HMI Primary Survey. But how? The heads who responded saw a variety of possibilities which focussed on three areas of function: clear and unequivocal support by the head and senior staff for the efforts of teachers with posts of responsibility; the enhancement of their professional knowledge through attendance at courses, visits to other schools, scope to improve their qualifications and more time in school to carry out their duties; and through the provision of better salaries and of good promotion prospects.

Status was seen by the heads as a differential opportunity. On the one hand as support and inducement for the teacher with a post of responsibility. On the other hand, the teacher with a post of responsibility is expected to be well-informed, to have gained the post by merit and be readily able to accept the responsibility which enhanced status demands. It is thus that the teacher with the post of responsibility will gain the genuine support of the head and the respect of his colleagues. But this is perhaps to over-simplify the range of possibilities through which the heads could see means for enhancing the status of post-holders. The following will give some indication of the diversity of views expressed:

Create devolution of responsibility in the school.

Make others aware of the duties of post-holders.

Provide an agreed job description.

Head's attitude of respect for post-holders is essential.

Recognition of work done.

Give opportunity and resources for post-holders to develop their expertise.

Increase promotion prospects.

Appoint only those with additional qualifications.

What is not clear from the heads' responses is the feasibility of each possible means for enhancing the standing of post-holders. Each carries with it potential costs as well as potential benefits. Some are no more than palliatives of short-term value. Others may require considerable structural changes. It is however the case that heads considered in very positive terms, that enhanced status for post-holders is possible, though one head considered that the appointment of fewer teachers to posts of responsibility could lead to the same end.

The training requirement

Some sixty per cent of the heads considered it desirable for teachers with posts of responsibility to undertake a course of training. Forty per cent did not. Those who did, considered that the content of such training should be in, and by exposure to:

a) curriculum development work or a curriculum area;
b) such management skills as leadership, communication, monitoring and resource allocation;
c) new educational ideas and practices; their philosophy and theory.

Heads emphasized some areas more than others, though training in management skills was considered important by many. Knowledge of research findings, methods of assessment and evaluation as well as of accountability were mentioned, as was the need to provide for the kind of training which was grounded in practical experience.

Most heads saw local authorities and their advisers as having an important role to play in training. Colleges and universities were not seen to have a large part to play, though teachers' centres were mentioned. Some heads saw themselves making a contribution to training and many considered that training should be broadly school-based. In one instance, the onus for training was considered to be the responsibility of the individual teacher.

Chain of responsibility

Thirty-three heads said post-holders should be responsible to them. Eighteen others to the head and the staff jointly. Two heads included parents with themselves and the staff. Others said 'Head and senior staff', 'Head and your year leader' and 'Head and head of department'. But quite evidently most heads considered that post-holders were responsible to them, completely or in large part. One head noted: ' . . . though democracy is important' and one that, 'HMIs and advisers should be more involved.' Another two indicated that it was to the whole school that the post-holder was responsible and a further two that: 'It's (the school's) philosophy' which had a part to play.

The heads, as one would expect from their assumption of responsibility for the work of post-holders, see themselves as major monitoring agents either alone or with senior staff; at staff meetings or together with advisers. They also note a range of more or less objective methods for monitoring the performance of post holders:

weekly reports –
regular reviews –
collective observation –
in-depth discussion –
assessment of children's progress.

Such methods, it should be pointed out, are not to be taken as inquisitorial; they are, as one head put it, 'a critical examination of performance in a supportive situation'. The other side of the coin, as several heads noted, was the need to establish relevant educational criteria based on agreed goals to inform the methods employed to monitor the performance of post-holders. Job descriptions and evaluation documents would also need to reflect relevant criteria. However, there was the head who said, 'Mine is a small school where everyone knows everyone. No monitoring is needed.' It may be that such sentiments apply widely to the intimate setting not only of small schools but also of small departments.

Appointment of post-holders

Over seventy per cent of the heads said they were in general agreement with present practices in appointing teachers to posts of responsibility. Some of the heads who approved of the present practice of appointing post-holders, though they were not asked to do so, gave their reasons which may be summed up in the following comments:

Yes, I like to be able to see a teacher at work in his own school.

Yes, the head can assess the school's needs and satisfy them by appointment from present staff or through advertisement and interview.

and

Yes, because I have not discovered a better method.

Of those heads who were not in agreement with the present methods of appointing post-holders, several gave as their reason the lack of adequate job descriptions and the need for an improved definition of 'responsibility'. Several others commented on the lack of liaison between themselves and advisers in making appointments to posts of responsibility. Others commented on the too frequent use of 'length of service' as the main criterion of appointment. Two other comments are worth noting for the light which they shed on the ways in which appointment practices might be improved:

> Teachers seeking a post of responsibility for subject areas try to make themselves fit the advert. Yet they have little training in the subject. This makes it difficult to ascertain how proficient they are.

and

> The present system discourages those members of staff who have particular skills to share their expertise unless they have a specific post.

The fuller use of teacher expertise

The heads' response to the suggestion made in the HMI Survey that fuller use of teachers' particular strengths would make their expertise more generally available, was to welcome it. Over eighty per cent of them considered the suggestion either an excellent one or a good one generally, but posing some difficulties. Fewer than ten per cent of the heads thought that it was an idea likely to cause more harm than good. Heads who most welcomed the suggestion gave as their reasons that it would lead to an improvement in the esteem of many teachers, increase their professional involvement and attitudes and reduce the frustration of the present static promotions position. One head endorsed the suggestion as an excellent one: 'Because it works in this school' and another because: 'A good example is better than a lot of theory.' One head cautioned: 'To work well it (the suggestion) would need to involve a large number of teachers to cover all areas.' However, these heads tended to endorse the suggestion partly because, for one reason or another, it was already happening and partly because of the probability that it would result in professionally desirable responses leading to higher levels of teaching competence. Also, in one instance, perhaps an important one, that its implementation 'would help change the attitude that scale 1 is a failure scale'.

Those heads who endorsed the suggestion but saw some difficulties, considered that conflict with post-holders might arise over who should be the source of advice, and with senior staff, over views about teaching and assessing. However, the general endorsement was based on the development of the combined expertise of the teaching staff of the school and the opportunity of teachers to contribute more widely than just as class teachers.

Heads not well disposed to the suggestion thought that it would lower the status of post-holders, might lead to 'interference' in the work of other colleagues, to teachers trying to demonstrate how 'promotion-worthy' they were and to the resentment of older teachers. Practical difficulties were also raised: the need for training, releasing teachers to make their expertise available and to the over-organization of young teachers by 'teacher experts'.

General comments

The general comments made by heads ranged widely, though there were two issues to which they frequently referred. These were the problem of 'inherited' staff and the need to restructure the salary scale to fit the changed staffing circumstance of the primary school so that the 'expert' class teacher is retained in the classroom.

The other comments referred to the need for every school to have the maximum number of posts of responsibility; that appointments to such posts should be in terms of generally accepted guidelines; or a clear job description. There were also comments on the wider use of teacher expertise, focussing largely on the need for staff to be engaged in a common enterprise: to cooperate as a team, perhaps through small committees coordinated by staff with special curricular interests, and so to generate professional involvement and boost morale.

Some heads did caution against the too close definition of the role of the teacher 'expert' whether awarded a post of responsibility or not, and one head wrote: 'There is something to be said for awarding scale posts for simply being a very good class teacher as against the whiz kid holding a post for A.V.A. or resources management.' It is the sentiment that is conveyed in this comment that permeates many of the views expressed by the heads. They also appreciate that some very able teachers would not function well as post-holders, or 'experts' making their advice generally available, either because they lack the necessary personal qualities or the right training.

Some heads saw management problems as a consequence of widening teacher responsibility: 'It would be necessary to clarify differences between using the skills of non-post-holders and the responsibilities of a specified post of responsibility', stated one head. Other heads could foresee problems of status and reward, of an experience-inexperience conflict. As one head put it: '"Volunteers" might resent the "paid hands".' However, the general impression was of heads prepared to confront the issues raised by posts of responsibility, their nature and function and the need to make more generally available the expertise of all teachers and to confront the issues in an open and fair-minded way.

Summing up: the evidence of the heads

A summing up is essentially a stance in relation to the evidence. The stance adopted here is that each primary school is a unique organism with a life of its own, adapting and responding daily to the issues that confront it. What each primary school shares with all other primary schools is a commitment to primary education and a striving towards those educational aims which fit its own circumstances and legitimately make it a primary school. It follows from this that any general commentary on what the heads have said may be taken to fit the circumstances of a particular school, or not, as the case may be. It also follows, or should do, that every primary school will respond within itself to the issues raised by the evidence arising from the data of the Heads' Questionnaire.

The first – and perhaps the most important – issue is that of extending the opportunity for every teacher within a school to make a valid contribution to the pool of expertise available for the development of its curriculum. This is both in terms of what *could be* and what *is* taught within the school, in a setting where the head sees himself largely, if not entirely responsible for the character and quality of the curriculum, and where some teachers are paid to undertake responsibility for certain areas of teaching. Heads appear generally well disposed to the suggestion that wider use should be made of the expertise of every teacher, yet they also see problems arising from such a development. Not least, though this is not overtly stated, they are concerned about the control and effects of the fuller use of the expertise of all teachers on their staff. This concern may be very real. The acquisition of expertise in teaching comes not only from practice and experience in teaching, but also from a developed awareness of the wider curricular context of one's work. Teachers may need to be made more aware of this context than they are, of its roots and its educational purposes. Moreover, they may need to be trained to analyse the adequacy of new curricular proposals and proposed changes in teaching methods.

Teachers may need to be trained, not only those with posts of responsibility but all teachers, to appreciate the nature of the expertise to which they may legitimately lay claim. Most heads accept the need to provide training for teachers with posts of responsibility especially in curriculum areas, in management skills and in a critical awareness of new educational ideas and practices. Not one head however, expressed the opinion that many teachers may well need some training in the best use of human resources of the school if the optimum use of the expertise of all teachers is to be achieved. Until issues of this kind are confronted it is not possible to know which are the best agencies to carry them out. The heads tend to prefer training, whoever it is for, to be kept close to the school, to involve themselves, though they accept that LEA advisers may have a vital role to play. It may well be that 'in-house-training' is the best way to cope with what is after all largely awareness (and maybe assertion) training. The proposition needs to be tested.

It is also the case that the giving (and even the taking) of advice, if it is to be optimally successful, requires special skills of communicating and relating to one's peers. Not everyone has, or can develop, these skills. It may well be a case of horses for courses. If so, then the suggestion made by the Primary Survey that teachers' particular strengths should be put to fuller use by making their expertise more generally available by giving them responsibility for an area of the curriculum, needs to be taken cautiously. This is exactly the warning given by some heads.

However, the generally favourable view of the head teachers to the idea of making fuller use of the curricular strengths of their colleagues, suggests that despite the difficulties which might attend such a development, it is worth pursuing.

Also worth pursuing, and arising from the heads' 'evidence' is the role and function of teachers with scale posts of responsibility. The issue is whether their efforts should be in the direction of innovation and change or conservation and development; between raising the curricular dynamics of the school or maintaining the curricular qualities of what is already achieved. Some heads can be said to take a *tough-minded* stance toward the qualities to be sought after in scale post-holders – exceptional teaching ability, subject and curriculum knowledge and good qualifications together with the readiness to accept responsibility, assert authority and lead. Others take a *tender-minded* stance emphasizing good classroom skill, proven competence, wide experience and long service to the school together with loyalty, a compatible philosophy, empathy with the needs of the school, tact, amicability, congeniality and keenness.

Some heads, of course, appear to take a professional stance toward the qualities of post-holders. They want 'enthusiasm, drive, verve, energy and initiative' but harnessed to new ideas in education, an interest in new possibilities in primary education, a willingness to attend courses and to learning more about curriculum development – and they want these qualities to function in an open, supportive but critical atmosphere.

Whatever the case, there is sufficient evidence to warrant an examination of the concept of posts of responsibility both in terms of the qualities needed to discharge the post effectively and of what post-holders should be aiming to do. There were also sufficient negative comments to suggest that in some schools such posts, if not an incubus, are at least a telling constraint on curricular developments.

Neither better job specification, which some heads seek, nor improved role clarity and support from the head and senior staff, may be sufficient to raise the standing of teachers with posts of responsibility; especially where so little time is available in most schools for the exercise of responsibility. What may be needed is nothing less than a reappraisal of what responsibilities need to be discharged throughout the school under currently restricted circumstances, to ensure that the highest possible quality of educational life is lived in the school for those whom it serves: its pupils and the community. At least this would seem to follow from the analysis of the freely offered comments of the heads. It is to the opinions of the teachers that we now turn.

Teachers respond

The questionnaire

The aim of the questionnaire to teachers was to parallel that completed by heads and to sample their views on which functions and activities *should* be discharged by holders of posts of responsibility, both paid and unpaid; also to discover what functions a post-holder *actually* performed and with what frequency. In addition the questionnaire sought to gather teachers' opinions about the HMI proposal that fuller use of the curricular and teaching strengths of *all* teachers could be made more generally available by giving every teacher responsibility for an aspect of the curriculum. The questionnaire also asked for the views of teachers about the kind of training required for undertaking a post of responsibility, and on the possible consequences of implementing a policy to encourage the wider use of teacher expertise in the primary school. Central to the questionnaire was the issue of which curriculum areas and on what activities within these areas would teachers wish to seek advice and help from other teachers. In short, what expertise would they seek to draw upon from amongst their colleagues. A preliminary section of the questionnaire asked for a range of professional information – length of teaching experience, post held, age group taught and professional qualifications acquired, as well as teachers' views on desirable areas of teaching competence among primary school teachers and the degree of importance they would attach to sources of professional development. Finally, in this first section teachers with paid posts of responsibility were asked to state their current area of responsibility; how, when they were awarded the post, they were advised of its nature; how much time, both in and out of school they devoted to the discharge of their responsibility and whether they thought their skills and their time were or were not used to advantage.

Sampling of schools

Seventy schools were involved in the study and were part of a careful process of sampling which aimed to produce a spectrum of school types – infant, junior, junior/infant, first and middle – as well as schools of varying sizes ranging from large schools with over 350 children on roll to small schools with fewer than 250 children on the roll. Not every school drawn in the sample responded to the invitation to participate in the study, though some 65 per cent did so.

The responding teachers

A total of 465 teachers responded to the questionnaire, of whom 364 were women and 101 men. About half of the teachers, 280, had been teaching for more than ten years and just less that 20 per cent for five years or less. The great majority of the teachers were college trained and held a teacher's certificate. Some 60 per cent held paid posts of responsibility exclusive of those who were deputy heads (some 11 per cent). Very few teachers held designated, unpaid posts of responsibility – twenty in all. The teachers were distributed across the whole range of teaching – nursery to upper juniors. A minority of them, around 20 per cent were members of a teaching association other than a union.

The presumed competence of primary school teachers

Most teachers considered that they and their colleagues would be 'fully' competent in only two curriculum areas:

　　Mathematics (93.4 per cent)
　　Reading and Language Skills (98.7 per cent)

and partially competent (or rather more so) in the remaining seven areas:

　　Science (92.7 per cent)
　　Music (73.5 per cent)

Art and craft (95 per cent)
Physical education and games (93.4 per cent)
Geography, history and social studies (92.2 per cent)
Religious education (80.4 per cent)
Environmental studies (95.1 per cent)

In general, the majority of teachers responding saw the need for a primary school teacher to possess a good degree of competence across a wide range of curriculum areas. Only in music and religious education did a substantial minority (26.6 per cent and 19.6 per cent) see little or no need for such competence. This is an understandable view in music which is taught in many primary schools by a specialist teacher, but worrying in religious education which is hardly anywhere taught by specialist teachers.

Perceived sources of professional development

Seven of the ten sources of professional development were seen as 'very' or 'extremely' important. In order they were:

Help from colleagues with special knowledge and experience (89.7 per cent)

Guidance from the head teacher (89.1 per cent)

Help from teachers with scale posts of responsibility (82.6 per cent)

Support from school based in-service courses (72.5 per cent)

Help from sympathetic colleagues – ideas from textbooks and teachers' guides (62.6 per cent)

Support from the local advisory service or the inspectorate (63.8 per cent)

Of significantly lesser importance were:

Ideas from the professional literature (42.8 per cent)

Information and suggestions from national reports and surveys (35.6 per cent)

Support from the professional literature (30.5 per cent)

Quite evidently the most significant locus of perceived professional development is to be found in the school, with its collegial group of head, deputy and staff.

Teachers with posts of responsibility

Table 2 below shows for which areas the 282 post-holders were responsible. Many were responsible for more than one area of the curriculum. The teaching and curriculum areas (a and b), together with responsibility for the resources supporting these areas (d) were the major areas of responsibility. Those concerned with an aspect of school organization or administration (e) and pastoral care (f) were minor areas of responsibility, attracting fewer posts.

Table 2: Teachers having responsibility for designated areas

Area of responsibility	*No.t's*
a) Responsibility for teaching a particular subject, e.g. music, physical education, reading, science	138
b) Responsibility for a curriculum area, e.g. language, mathematics etc.	127
c) Responsibility for teaching a particular group of children, e.g. those in need of remedial teaching, more able children	44
d) Responsibility for teaching materials and/or resources, e.g. textbooks or library books	129
e) Responsibility for an aspect of school organization or administration, e.g. management of stock, purchase of materials	106
f) Responsibility for the welfare of children, e.g. pastoral care	44
g) 'Other' areas not specified above	76

Among 'other' areas of responsibility were mentioned:

Head of infant and/or nursery departments (4)*
Curriculum coordination (3)
Corridor display and display throughout the school (7)
Running the school bookshop (3)
Chess club
As senior mistress, giving advice to less experienced
colleagues (2)
Team leader
Assessment of reading (2)
Standing in for the Head
First aid
Year group coordination or similar responsibility (14)
Netball team, swimming etc. (3)
Organization of special events e.g. school concert
School trips (3)
School assembly (3)
Liaison with infant or first school (2)
Head of department (4)
Timetable (2)
Running the school kitchen (1)
Secondary school liaison (2)
Liaison with parents (2)
Audiovisual aids (2)
Classifying reading materials (1)
Handwriting (1)

In addition to the above there were ten mentions of deputy heads –
many, as one would expect, with a very considerable range of
responsibilities associated with their role. Clearly, as well as the
broadly defined areas of responsibility there were many other
specific areas of responsibility, all necessary in some degree to the
well being of a primary school.

When asked what advice they had been given about the nature of
their responsibilities, three-quarters of the post-holders said

---

* The numbers in brackets indicate the total number of times an area of
responsibility was mentioned.

'informally' and 'verbally', and half said 'in general terms'. Some 70 per cent said they would have wished to have had more information regarding their responsibilities. The kind of information they wished for ranged from information about the kind of decision that should be referred to the head, to the request for more information about the school's basic educational philosophy. In fifteen instances a written account of the responsibilities was the kind of information desired, and in a further twenty-six instances greater specificity, clarity, detail and exactness of duties was asked for. One respondent wrote: 'Any little crumb of information would have been useful' and another, 'I have developed the job much as I wanted, but the base was "woolly".' Others were concerned to know where the responsibilities started and where they ended, and one teacher who thought she had responsibility for one particular area of the curriculum found that she had other responsibilities about which she had been told nothing.

In fact almost one-third (89 out of 288) of the teachers with posts of responsibility expressed a desire for more information about their posts. Even so, most post-holders felt that their skills and time were more or less used to full capacity, though for more than half, less than a quarter of their time *in school* was given over to the discharge of responsibilities. Out of school, teachers with posts of responsibility claimed that they spent anything from little or no time to as much as 25 hours on their responsibilities.

About half (144) the teachers with posts of responsibility said that they spent up to five hours of their own time on activities relating to their posts, and a further 111 said they spent between five and nine hours. Some 10 per cent of the teachers (32) spent ten hours or more of their own time on activities related to their posts of responsibility. Several stated that they spent twenty hours or more, and some teachers that the amount of their own time which they spent was 'variable'.

Teachers' views on the functions and activities that teachers with posts of responsibility should undertake

It is abundantly clear from the responses that teaching and curriculum responsibilities, together with the provision of necessary support resources, are the activities *most* teachers would endorse as those in which teachers with posts of responsibility should primarily involve themselves – though, as will be seen, not to the exclusion of other activities. The most heavily endorsed activities were:

2:1a)   Teaching a particular subject to classes that are not 'their own'

2:2a)   Maintaining and developing teaching resources in an area of the curriculum for general use in the school

2:1g)   Keeping an eye on work in a particular area of the curriculum

2:1n)   Teaching children whose first language is not English

2.2d)   Managing library books and other resources

In addition to these activities, caring for sick children and pastoral care were activities in which teachers with posts of responsibility were expected to engage. The activities which teachers with posts of responsibility were generally expected to engage in *least* were:

2:1j)   Chairing a group of colleagues working in a curriculum area

2:1b)   Demonstrating a lesson or teaching method for their colleagues

2:4c)   Organizing an event for a group of children on behalf of a colleague, e.g. a school visit

2:1i)   Testing or screening for grouping or setting children

2:4b)   Organizing an event for the school, e.g. parents' evening, meeting of PTA etc.

A more comprehensive picture of those areas of activity which were expected to occupy the time of teachers with posts of responsibility can be seen in Table 3 below. This gives the mean frequency for the four main categories of activities used in the questionnaire.

From this table it is plain that the responding teachers consider that their colleagues with posts of responsibility, whether paid or not, should be generally more involved in teaching and curriculum, resource and welfare related activities than in administration and organizing activities. However, the range of responsibilities was wide. Under the heading 'Other Responsibilities' the responding teachers noted the following:

Organizing games and matches (5)*

Management of stock (4)

Display (2)

In-service courses (2)

Whole school activities e.g. concerts, taking assembly, discipline, yard and dinner duty, fire drill etc. (3)

Communication between staff (2)

Care of individual children e.g. in sick bay, monitoring progress of students on school or community service (4)

most of which fall outside the categories employed in the questionnaire. One which was noted, though not mentioned, 'staff room morale', might well be considered to be more than the responsibility of any single member of staff.

Table 3:   Mean frequency of activities considered desirable for teachers with posts of responsibility

Activities	*Mean*
Teaching and curriculum	3.23
Resource	3.39
Welfare and liaison	3.46
Administrative and organizing	2.63

The fuller use of the expertise of the primary school teacher

The suggestion contained in the HMI Survey, *Primary Education in England*, that fuller use of teachers' particular strengths in areas of the curriculum would be achieved by making their expertise more generally available, was explored in this section of the questionnaire. This was done firstly by asking the responding

---

*　Figures in brackets indicate the frequency of mention.

teachers in which of nine curriculum areas they thought that class teachers would wish to draw on the expertise of their colleagues. Secondly, by asking them about the possible effects of the wider use of teacher expertise. Thirdly, by asking what expertise should be on offer and finally by asking them on what the efficient use of teacher expertise would depend.

Drawing on the expertise of colleagues

Teachers were asked to what extent – 'very much', 'to some extent' and 'not at all' – they thought class teachers would wish to draw on the expertise of their colleagues in nine curriculum areas under four headings:

Preparing schemes of work.

Advising on teaching methods.

Advising on methods of assessment.

Managing resources.

Table 4 overleaf gives a quantified result; the lower the figure the less are the class teachers considered likely to want to draw on the expertise of their colleagues for a specific expertise; the higher, the more likely.

The broad picture emerging from the responses was that primary school teachers might well wish to draw on the expertise of their colleagues for advice on preparing schemes of work, advice on teaching methods and on managing resources. Also – but to a significantly lesser extent – for advice on methods of assessment. The curriculum areas in which advice is most likely to be sought are mathematics, science, music and language and reading skills; to a lesser extent in physical education and games, arts and crafts, environmental studies, topic work, history, geography and hardly at all in religious education. Speaking generally, there was evidence of a good level of expressed readiness on the part of class teachers to draw on the expertise of their colleagues.

Table 4:

Curriculum area	Areas of Expertise				
	Preparing schemes of work	Advising on teaching methods	Advising on methods of assessment	Managing resources	Overall mean
Mathematics	2.69	2.33	2.34	2.18	2.38
Science	2.68	2.38	2.11	2.33	2.37
History, geography, social studies	2.33	1.96	1.82	1.99	2.02
Religious ed.	2.24	1.86	1.64	1.79	1.88
Music	2.64	2.46	2.06	2.27	2.36
Language and reading skills	2.68	2.40	2.45	2.24	2.44
Art and craft	2.32	2.18	1.78	2.15	2.11
Environmental studies and topic work	2.31	2.01	1.82	2.02	2.04
PE and games	2.39	2.20	1.86	2.09	2.13
Overall mean	2.48	2.19	1.99	2.12	

The possible effects of the wider use of teacher expertise

The results from the next part of the questionnaire which sought teachers' views on the possible effects of the wider use of the expertise of teachers amply confirm the earlier impression that class teachers in the primary school would be willing to draw on the expertise of their colleagues. Among the most strongly endorsed items were:

i)   All teachers in the primary school have special teaching talents and every effort should be made to use these throughout the school.

j)   Teachers in the primary school welcome help in areas of teaching where they are weak.

t)   Class teachers cannot be expected to cover all the areas of the primary school curriculum with equal confidence.

Also clearly endorsed were:

b)   The teacher with responsibility for a curriculum area is essential to sound educational practices in the primary school.

d)   No class teacher can expect to be able to cover *all* areas of the curriculum and so provide an effective education.

g)   The teacher with special responsibility for a curriculum area is an essential resource in the primary school.

k)   Class teachers in the primary school need help and advice in planning schemes of work.

In addition the value of giving responsibility for teaching a subject rather than a class (1)* was recognized. Also that teachers would readily seek advice from a colleague with a clearly designated responsibility for a curriculum area (q) and that teachers were more likely to seek advice about the curriculum than advice on teaching it (r).

---

*   Letters in brackets refer to specific items in appropriate sections of the questionnaire.

However, it must be emphasized that the endorsement of both the use of teachers' expertise and the need for its availability in curricular matters in no way eroded the general value to be placed on paid posts of responsibility, not only as a stage in a teaching career but also as necessary to the effective running of a primary school. Furthermore, the more general use of teacher expertise was not seen as a threat to class teaching nor likely to lead to the fragmentation of learning.

The key to such a positive appreciation of the wider use of the expertise of teachers may well reside in the very strong endorsement of:

s)   Informal (rather than formal) contact between teachers facilitates the asking and giving of advice.

and the very weak endorsement of:

f)   Only under the guidance of an 'expert' is it possible for children to understand certain areas of the curriculum.

Teachers would seem to welcome the opportunity to seek support from their colleagues given that the wider use of teacher expertise is part of the informal system of the primary school, is confined to curricular matters and that a healthy scepticism about expertise is exercised.

What expertise on offer?

In reply to the question '. . . in which of the following curriculum areas and activities do you believe primary school teachers will have expertise to offer?', one area of expertise was outstanding – b) Practical experience of the classroom. Other areas and activities in which more than 'a fair amount' of expertise would be available were:

a)   Knowledge in an academic subject.

c)   Understanding of human relations.

h)   Knowledge of social relations in school and classroom.

j) Understanding of teaching techniques.

k) Skills needed for developing schemes of work.

n) Organizational skills.

o) Knowledge of how children learn.

It was believed that teachers would *not* have management and administrative skills (d), nor skills in debate and discussion (m), or in handling meetings or working parties (p) to offer to any but a small extent. Nor would there be any but minimal experience of teaching at more than one level of education (r) on which to draw.

The results of this part of the questionnaire are, in some degree, surprising. Teachers would appear to have considerable expertise to offer in an area, practical experience of the classroom, which might well not be sought by their colleagues. However, it is evident that primary school teachers are believed, by their colleagues, to have considerable expertise to offer in many areas on which they could and would draw; it is mainly practical experience rather than theory that they have to offer. Even so, knowledge of the theory of teaching (item 1) was considered by 77 per cent of the teachers to be an area of expertise on offer more than 'somewhat' by primary school teachers in general.

The teacher expert in action

The next issue dealt with in the questionnaire was just how the teacher 'expert' should function. In the best interests of the expert's school (a), the children in it (d) and of primary education (b) were thought to be important criteria that should govern the work of the teacher 'expert'. As important was the readiness of the teacher 'expert' to share his professional knowledge with his colleagues (j) and extend his field of interests beyond his own subject (i). A ready acceptance of suggestions and criticism was also seen as desirable (k). Other characteristics and qualities noted were seen as only a little less desirable: awareness of innovation in primary education (f), attending to necessary changes in teaching (g), awareness of the recommendations of national reports and support for the professional development of his colleagues were all endorsed 'to some extent' as 'worthwhile' attributes and functions of the teacher 'expert'.

Only the exclusive concentration on his own area of responsibility within the school was seen as an undesirable trait of the teacher 'expert'! It is clear that as innovator, change agent and curricular resource, the teacher 'expert' is expected to function in the interests of his school, its children and his colleagues.

Efficient use

To 'a great extent' the efficient use of the teacher expert was judged to depend upon the degree of support given by the head and senior staff of the school (l), the degree to which the school has thought through its aims (j) and the length and relevance of their own teaching experience (d). Other factors such as a clear and explicit sphere of responsibility (i), the level of financial and other resources available to the teacher 'expert' (h), the emphasis the school gives to monitoring and standards (k), the degree of access to the head and senior staff (e) as well as the status the teacher 'expert' is accorded by his colleagues (a) were also considered of consequence in the efficient use of the teacher 'expert'. The efficient use of the teacher 'expert' is quite clearly seen to be rooted not only in general collegial support but also in certain institutional characteristics of the school, in particular its concern for standards and the clarity of its aims.

Training – in which field?

If there is to be training for the teacher 'expert', then, *par excellence*, teachers considered it should be in a curriculum area (b). Almost 85 per cent endorsed this field of training. Training in the assessment of children's capabilities (i), in organization and administration (d), and in remedial work (f) were also considered desirable by a large proportion of teachers (over 65 per cent). Knowledge of the education of high ability children (h) and of diagnostic tests (j) were also two areas of training considered desirable, but to a lesser extent. Between 60 and 65 per cent of the teachers endorsed those fields of training. The two least endorsed areas were transition to primary education (g) and environmental studies (c).

Consequences

What would result from the development of the teacher 'expert' in the primary school? This was the final question posed in the questionnaire and answered in terms of 'likely', or 'very likely', 'unlikely' or 'very unlikely'. The statements most endorsed as 'likely' and 'very likely' taken together were:

l) greater demand for in-service courses (90.7 per cent)
b) higher standards of teaching (73.6 per cent)
g) an improved educational base for primary education (72.4 per cent)
i) a greater economy of teaching resources (67.4 per cent)
h) a fairer distribution of teaching load (57.9 per cent)
c) a general rise in the morale of staff (53.1 per cent)

All very desirable outcomes of a policy to encourage the wider use of teacher expertise in the primary school. However, a significant proportion of teachers considered that implementation of such a policy would result in: f) an increase in morale *only* of those teachers designated 'expert' (48 per cent of teachers thought such an outcome 'likely' or 'very likely'). But this was thought to be the only negative result of the implementation of such a policy. It was *not* thought generally likely that the policy would lead to a fragmentation of children's curricular experience, higher standards *only* in basic subjects, lack of balance in the curriculum, less job satisfaction for primary school teachers, the readier control of the primary school by the LEA and the State, less individual learning nor the erosion of class teaching – though in every instance a minority of between 30 and 40 per cent of teachers thought such an outcome possible.

But teachers see things differently

It is not unreasonable to be sceptical about statistics and to argue that averages and percentages conceal differences; they do, and it is these differences that we now aim to explore. The picture so far presented is *true* of the *general* run of primary school teacher in the sample but there were differences between teachers on some of the issues presented in the questionnaire and it is important to examine these if as true a picture of teachers' opinions as possible is to be arrived at.

*Attitudes to the wider use of teacher expertise**

Two viewpoints emerged from an analysis of the variations among the responses of the teachers to the 26 statements about the nature of teaching in the primary school and the possible effects of a policy to make wider use of teacher expertise. One came from a strong endorsement of the values of class teaching and the continuity and stability that it offered. The other from a belief in the virtues of teacher and subject organization. Teachers of younger children, and, as you would expect, teachers in infant schools, women teachers and more experienced teachers, tended to support the first point of view – that class teaching is important to a sound education in the primary school – while younger teachers, teachers of older children, especially teachers in middle schools and most particularly, teachers who were members of a teaching association other than a union, supported the virtues of teacher and subject specialization. A third, but less marked point of view concerned the value of posts of responsibility. Some teachers supported them. Some did not. There were, however, no systematic differences to account for the opposing view. In fact there was evidence of ambivalence with the same teacher agreeing with the suggestion that they should be abolished *and* with the proposition that such posts offer opportunity for promotion.

Views on 'expertise' on offer

One form of expertise which teachers have to offer is *professional knowledge* and understanding – knowledge of children, how they

---

*   Appendix 4 consists of data derived from factor analysis on which some of this section is based.

learn, of effective teaching and the purposes teaching is intended to serve. The availability of such expertise is emphasized in the main by all teachers, though most particularly by teachers without posts of responsibility, by teachers of younger children and by women teachers.

Teachers with posts of responsibility (including deputy heads) tend – as one might expect – to lay greater store by managerial expertise and practical skills outside the classroom – skill in handling meetings, in debate and discussion as well as administrative skills.

There is a further form of expertise – in techniques of value in curriculum development, especially that which is close to the realities and needs of the classroom. This form of expertise is widely valued by all primary school teachers, irrespective of status, experience or level of responsibility.

How should the teacher expert function?

One way teachers had of seeing the teacher 'expert' was as an agent of change, alert to innovations in primary education and determined to make a contribution to the professional development of his colleagues. Another, as a quietly concerned colleague, ready to help if asked to. In the main it was the last way of seeing the teacher 'expert' that was most generally supported. The former found more support among teachers with posts of responsibility and among teachers who belong to a teaching association. But this support, though evident, was not strong.

Summing up

Facts do not speak for themselves and as they have been presented in the foregoing sections, they have been commented on. What is offered now is a brief resume by way of summing up, and a pulling together of what appear to be reasonably connected strands.

1   Teachers see themselves and their colleagues as having competence in a broad range of curriculum areas, most particularly

in mathematics and reading and language skills. It is for responsibility in these areas that many teachers hold scaled posts, and it is generally considered that teachers with posts of responsibility should do so, though not to the exclusion of other areas of responsibility.

2   Although teachers see themselves and their colleagues as competent in a wide range of curriculum areas, especially in mathematics and reading and language skills, they express a readiness to draw on the expertise of their colleagues in many curriculum areas and most especially in those areas in which they feel themselves to be most competent – with the exception of music in which they acknowledge only some competence. However, it is not expertise in teaching which they seek but in preparing schemes of work and to a lesser extent for advice on methods of assessment.

3   Teachers with scale posts figure prominently among those sources of professional development valued by teachers. So do heads and colleagues. In fact it is the collegial, informal system that teachers endorse as valid and most likely to facilitate the giving and taking of advice.

4   There is no rejection of the need for posts of responsibility in curriculum areas. They are seen as essential to sound educational practices in the primary school. However, it is clear that primary school teachers have expertise which they believe ought to be available for use in the schools in which they teach, and this ranges widely across a variety of professional skills.

5   If expertise is to be available, then teachers see that its efficient use depends upon support from the head and senior staff, the clarity of a school's aims and on the availability of training – espcially in relevant areas of the curriculum.

6   The consequences of making wider use of the expertise of teachers, not only those with posts of responsibility but also of those who hold no such posts, were generally seen as positive, raising standards of teaching and of professional awareness.

Additional evidence

As well as the questionnaires to heads and to teachers, discussions were held with groups of heads and teachers, diaries were kept by some teachers with posts of responsibility for a short period of time noting their interactions with colleagues and yet other teachers, also with posts of responsibility, produced guided 'free accounts' of what holding a post of responsibility entailed. Here we will summarize the main points which came out of these three explorations.

The groups*

The groups, three of them, one of which was mixed, are mainly of post-holders and one was solely of heads. The mixed groups were all class teachers, some with and some without posts of responsibility. Each group was asked to discuss the nature of posts of responsibility, their effectiveness, the constraints encountered, the need for training, the kind of expertise on which the average primary school teacher might wish to draw. Of course many other related issues came up in what were frequently vigorous discussions.

Functions of the teacher 'expert': role and job description

The group of heads produced as a result of their discussions – and as one might expect from a group of people used to making administrative decisions – a very clear prospectus for the job of the teacher 'expert'. It was in order of priority:

1   *Teaching* his own class new topics, other classes complex topics, other classes jointly, his colleagues' complex topics, or principles of new equipment, withdrawal groups (e.g. gifted), parents' evenings . . .
2   *Drafting* schemes of work, summaries of staff discussions own job specification, assessment procedures, resource index, in-service course summaries . . .
3   *Displaying* children's work with comments, available resources, potential resources, in-service courses . . .
4   *Purchasing* books, equipment, materials . . .
5   *Discussing* formally in staff meetings, with year groups, with

---

*   See Appendix 5 for a copy of the brief for the group discussions.

children (in front of staff), with LEA advisors, with head, with parents . . . Informally by request or by initiative with individual colleagues . . .

6   *Arranging* visits for children, visits for colleagues to other schools, particularly to attend in-service courses.

7   *Evaluating* children's work, children's progress, children's needs, also staff work, progress and needs . . .

Not, of course, that any of the 'experts' would or could be expected to cover all these areas of endeavour. Rather that all the activities needed to be covered in a well-run primary school. Every teacher expert's priority was nevertheless seen to be teaching his own class.

Most of the heads believed in job descriptions for the post of the teacher expert, at least in terms of the clarity with which the role was described when advertised; such advertisements should include some demands that went beyond successful practice in a curriculum area. They had in mind the ability to talk to staff meetings, to arrange exhibitions of teaching materials, to produce curricular guidelines, to monitor children's achievements and to be knowledgeable about children of all ages in the primary school.

A second group comprised mainly of teachers with posts of responsibility, reported that of the sixteen members of the group only three – all from the same school – had written job descriptions. These descriptions were in two sections – a general part that related to all post-holders and a part written specifically for a particular post. Copies of the job descriptions were given to all other members of staff. The group remarked that the question of what one actually did compared with what was expected of one, was difficult to assess in the absence of a written description. In the ensuing discussion the group explained what their responsibilities were and there was a large measure of argument between members, mainly from different schools, about the role of a teacher with a post of responsibility. They identified elements that enabled them to know 'what to do' in the absence of a written description. For example:

You respond to an ongoing assessment of need – that assessment is made in the light of your own experience.

You respond to demand – overt or covert – you feel the atmosphere.

> You know what is required of you by your initial training and on the job training.

> The job takes itself off – you just know where to start and what is needed.

They noted that there was very little direction from the head teacher either before the job or during. The general view of this group was that formal job descriptions were neither necessary nor helpful for the efficient performance of a post of responsibility.

The third group, who also consisted of post-holders, pinpointed some interesting facets of this issue of job specifications. Some had been appointed several years ago without having a job description and had been asked to write their own. These ranged from a simple title, for example, Mathematics, to a detailed description of the tasks the holder performed. Skimpy or detailed, they were received without comment.

It emerged from the discussions that many teachers were unaware of who was responsible for what area in their own school and also to what extent these people had 'authority' as holders of posts of responsibility. The consequent uncertainty, it was said, meant stepping very warily, always careful in personal contacts.

Training the teacher expert

Only the second group discussed this issue directly, though it was mentioned in passing by other groups. Most members of the group who discussed it felt themselves to have been sufficiently equipped for the posts they hold; unlike the members of the third group who indicated that some of them were given posts as recognition or reward for being conscientious teachers, but did not consider themselves 'specialists'. One was given a label 'Library' but in fact was awarded a post for work on teaching children to play the recorder.

Perhaps this was what was meant when the second group talked of training 'on the job'. They remarked that they had gained their training through assisting post-holders, and observing them at work, doing courses that were subject-related, or formed an element in their initial training. Necessary training was seen to consist of an across-schools (general) element and a school-specific element. The application of the general to the specific was seen to be central to the whole issue.

This group recommended that a greater measure of support from the LEA was necessary to enable teachers to attend courses in school time. The structure of the course should be such as to include discussions with other post-holders on areas lying outside any subject – for example, leadership, management and organizational skills – as well as in important curriculum areas. They also thought that use could be made of teachers with posts of responsibility, to run courses outside their own school.

Many of the problems relating to human relationships and the creation of a supportive climate for colleagues which were discussed in the third group's meetings, clearly stemmed from this lack of training, both in management skills and in 'subject expertise'. This third group was perceptive in remarking: 'How do we know that we need this help? We all think, because we are trained teachers, we are therefore expert.' Another commented on the lack of respect they felt for colleagues who held posts, but were not necessarily any more experienced or qualified than they were themselves.

Influence

The issue of the degree of influence that a teacher expert might be expected to exert in the school and on his colleagues was taken up very directly by the two teacher groups but only obliquely by the Heads. The nub of influence was clearly 'personal relationships'. It was around the functional mutuality of the need for support and the informality of how it was given that the power to influence became possible. It was also related to the climate and nature of the change that pervaded the school.

As Heads saw it, a minimal change could be a change of *resources* which may affect little else. However one should not undervalue the facilitating function of good resource maintenance – be it of the Library, the animal centre or the pottery. Change of *organization* is more pervasive as is change of *content*. Even more pervasive is a change of *teaching method*. Though the most pervasive change is to the *whole school atmosphere*. The inadequacy of superficial change is witnessed by the large number of resource packs now gathering dust in some primary school cupboards.

Since the most fundamental change is to the school's whole approach to its teaching, the role of the teacher expert is most likely to be successful when seen as part of the development of a school's whole approach to staff and curriculum development.

But in the teachers' view much change was merely transient. Several speakers claimed:

> . . . I was always going to someone for an idea . . . but it was a short-term thing . . . it'd give me an idea for say a project . . . or it filled up next week. It never really accumulated in any obvious sense, or really developed knowledge in that area, it was 'that'll fit in somewhere I'll do that' . . . it was nothing long term, it didn't develop any real professional expertise.

> . . . it's the lack of continuity, and I think this is what has to come out very strongly, this is where the experts now are having to look – a re-look at every subject of the curriculum, whether aims and objectives are done, how you are making the continuity from the seven-year-olds to the elevens . . . Teachers have been doing *bits* as you say . . .

Attempts to introduce fundamental root-and-branch changes which involved teachers with expert knowledge would, thought the heads, meet severe difficulties, not least the need to:

1 Re-negotiate posts of responsibility already allocated.
2 Make more time available for the major redevelopment of the work of the school needed *during the working day*.
3 Enhance the subject expertise of many primary school teachers in such subjects as mathematics, science, language and art.
4 Accept that genuine redevelopment of primary education is of its nature slow to mature.
5 Confront the issues of the generalist class teacher versus the subject specialist in a way that developed a consultative approach by every class teacher in recognition of an open professional pride not one that was exerted as of right and responsibility.

It is evident from this abridged account of the discussions by groups of teachers and heads that they are able to confront the issues raised by posts of responsibility and by the idea of the teacher experts. Equally it is evident that the post of responsibility in the primary school is a confused one. Finally, the way forward, whatever that may be, if it is radically to alter present practices may well meet stiff resistance not least because it will require the shedding of old assumptions about how responsibility and expertise is exercised and adopting new ones in circumstances where there is precious little time to reflect and where there is a tradition of existential engagement not of action as experiment to be proved by tested experience. It is such an issue as this that will be echoed in a later chapter.

Freely expressed

A small sample of thirty-five teachers, about half of whom were deputy heads and half scale two or scale three post-holders completed a schedule* asking them to say what holding a post of responsibility entailed.

The analysis of the free accounts showed that posts of responsibility called on the many strengths and varied talents of teachers. Often administrative and organizational responsibilities were combined with curriculum responsibilities and responsibility for accommodation and facilities.

The deputy head – 'piggy in the middle'

> My role is undocumented. I run the everyday business of the school, controlling timetables, capitation and day-to-day organization.

Examination of the free accounts revealed that a deputy head's role was very much influenced by the size of the school, the head of the school, their own individual talents and the various demands of the school environment. Each deputy head combined the duties of deputy head with other responsibilities. Their main duties,

---

* For a copy of the schedule see Appendix 6.

however, were to provide a link between the head and the staff and to be responsible for a wide range of routine (and occasional) matters – duty rotas, timetabling, disciplinary and pastoral affairs and such occasional matters as preparing for parents' evenings.

Most of the deputy heads were also responsible for a curriculum area, science, mathematics. On occasion such responsibilities could be considerable. One deputy head reported that his responsibility for science entailed: writing a science scheme and ensuring that it is being followed in school.

The picture that comes across from the free accounts is that the responsibilities of a deputy head involve those frustrations associated with being: 'a general oddjob man'. But there are rewards associated mainly with stimulating one's colleagues and there is always the hope (in some cases, the anticipation) of promotion.

However, several deputy headteachers pointed out that their role was at all times secondary to the responsibility for teaching the children in their classes. One deputy head stated that his 'main' responsibility was to his class and to each individual in it, not to his other responsibilities in the school, though clearly there was on occasion a conflict of obligations and at times sheer frustration at the trivia to be dealt with when, for example the head might want 'a quick word' over litter in the playground or a colleague wanted to know whether or not to ring the bell for 'a wet playtime'.

Scale post-holders

Some scale post-holders were responsible for coordinating the work of a year in the school, say, all first or second year work. For instance:

> As year coordinator I plan themes in consultation with the Head and 1st and 2nd year coordinators. I help a colleague who takes a parallel class to mine execute the plans and in consultation with them decide on programmes of work in various areas of the curriculum. I plan educational visits for children in the second year, and devise questionnaires. I am responsible for displaying work for second year sections in the corridor and the hall.

This teacher was also 'adviser for music' throughout the school!

A typical first year coordinator would oversee the running of the first year junior classes and deal with any difficulties and problems that arose: arrange meetings to deal with curriculum decisions and discuss work covered in class. At the end of the school year there would be liaison with staff concerning children moving on and the assessment of the new intake. Similarly, other year coordinators would find themselves responsible for a wide range of planning and curriculum functions *as well as* for teaching a class of children.

Despite what appear to be an impossible array of responsibilities to discharge, most of the teachers with scale posts for year coordination reported a high level of job satisfaction, probably because their roles were reasonably well-defined and possibly because their roles gave them visible status in the school and the eyes of their colleagues.

Post-holders with less well-defined responsibilities reported a lower level of satisfaction with their posts and frustration at the constraints imposed on their efforts by limitations of time and money. Among their duties were responsibilities for a range of curriculum areas – mathematics, art, drama, science, reading, dance, religious education, environmental studies and others. There were also other areas of responsibility – 'for resources', 'accommodation', 'display', 'first aid', 'library' and 'the bookshop'. In more than one case a teacher's post was for more than one area of responsibility.

Summing up

Teachers with posts of responsibility believed they were doing a good job, whether deputy head, year coordinator or scale post-holder. Most claimed that the lack of time, together with their primary responsibility as a class teacher made the discharge of their responsibilities at times difficult; at times frustrating. Even so it is clear from the teachers' accounts of their responsibilities, superficial as they may seem, that the discharge of responsibility adds significantly to the educational texture of life in the primary school.

The diaries*

Seven volunteers, all teachers with posts of responsibility, as well as full-time class teachers, kept diaries for a two-week period during the last half of a summer term. The diaries were loose-leaf with blank pages, so that diarists might record as much or as little as they needed, and only on the dates that they chose for themselves.

Any time in the school year is a bad time to keep a diary. At best the activity that goes on resembles Heathrow Airport at the height of the holiday season. It is quite surprising therefore that only one of the volunteers commented on the difficulty of completing a diary at this time in the school year and only partially responded.

The diaries that were fully completed reflected much of the bustle and intentness of schools, the meticulous attention to detail and occasionally to tensions and dramas.

Clearly many of the entries concerning long-term planning had their seeds sown months before – by whose hand, it would be hard to discover – a discreet word by the Head, a conference attended by both a teacher with a post of responsibility and Head, or a seemingly casual remark by a teacher may have been enough to prepare the ground. The diary merely recorded the steady growth in a school's activities or in some cases, the decision to prune them for financial reasons.

Many of the transactions recorded tended to reflect the tactical decisions and tasks that face most teachers whether post-holder or not. The setting up of equipment and its removal and the reminders of coming events appear to predominate. It would be hard to see how a diary could be kept that would not reflect such matters.

Time

One of the most frequently noted features was the lack of time allocated to staff with responsibility. Five of the seven diarists had to carry out all their duties entirely before or after school or during the breaks or in the dinner hour. The remaining two carried out most of their duties in this way, but were also 'subject specialists'

---

* See Appendix 7 for Diary Instructions

and were allocated time for teaching certain classes or groups, rather as a secondary teacher is timetabled. Most of the duties for taking and maintaining stock were done out of school. Staff frequently reported on regrading or sorting out material at home and on Sundays.

Music specialists noted that they not only advised on items of music, but frequently searched out and actually found the recording of a suitable item for another member of staff. This often entailed a visit to a local record library or similar resource centre at weekends.

Visits to resource centre, libraries, and consultations with others, such as librarians, all had to be accomplished either after school or on a Saturday. There could be no visits to other schools to see work in progress under this arrangement, and if at any time it should take place, special provision would have had to be made to cover their absence.

The encounters

The majority of the events recorded were of an informal nature, most of them occurring in the staffroom at break or dinner periods, others were noted as having taken place in the corridor.

Staff meetings were mentioned, but they tended to be omnibus events, dealing largely with impending organizational matters concerning the general running of the school, with an occasional curriculum item included – for example, the handing out of a scheme of work to the teachers present.

It is clear that primary schools necessarily have considerable time taken up with procedural matters. However, it is worth quoting at length the problems that do occur over curriculum matters. The following is a fairly typical example:

8.35 am Head's room.
Discussed staff meeting to take place next week in lunch hour (briefly). I consider half an hour insufficient time in which to achieve any significant thought or conclusions on multicultural education. I cannot see what Head expects to gain from it. A 'paper' was mentioned on the staff's conclusions. It would take a long time to achieve this. Tried to suggest this to the Head. The

Head does realize there will not be much achieved in the one meeting.

'10.00 – 10.30 staff room meeting.
Agenda:
a)   frieze in hall to be changed in time for parents' evening. Display boards allocated on multicultural theme.
b)   To discuss the new instructions for self-certifications.
c)   To consult staff about an entry for an art exhibition. Form has to be sent in immediately.

The average time taken over most encounters was two minutes and concerned requests for specific items such as white paint, a piece of music or a reading test, and occurred in the corridor or staffroom, mainly at break times.

Encounters about schemes of work ranged from long-term planning that had taken place over a number of months to the completion of earlier decisions, for example:

Discussion with the Head about the introduction of Scottish primary maths, into the junior department. This has been the ongoing discussion with all members of staff since the New Year. Decision is influenced by the organization of the age groups in the Junior dept. Decision to introduce the scheme (already working in the Infant department) into Junior 1 age group accepted by Head and myself in principle. A satisfactory encounter.

Same day, later that lunch time, encounter with Junior 1 teacher to report my discussion with Head. Teacher happy to go ahead with decision to introduce SMPG scheme in to Junior 1 in September.

or again in this example from another diarist:

Staff meeting 3.30 – 4.30.
My schemes of work for music were handed out.

It was clear that though the number of recorded instances where a post-holder is asked for help are few, they are not confined to the less experienced members of staff, as can be seen from the following.

Corridor 11.00. Instigation deputy head.
Deputy head asked me to set aside some time at the end of the summer term to discuss his approach to taking the bottom set for English (5 mins).

Following day class room break time.
Instigator deputy head.
Discussed the language and maths sets with deputy head.

Again the same diarist records a request for help but this time from a less experienced member of staff. Whilst informally asking for progress on the 'Young Reading Tests' with a first-year teacher, she was asked for advice on a child who had writing difficulties and requested a test. This discussion took ten minutes and was followed up the next day, when after school in the corridor the test was handed over to the teacher.

Discussions with the head teacher were by far the most numerous contacts recorded, ranging from receiving the go-ahead for the introduction of a scheme of work; one which had been under discussion for several months, over which the staff had been kept informed. In some cases, the specialist appeared to be more of a middle man, carrying out the wishes of the head revealed in the comment, 'will do as the head wishes – it's easier that way'.

From the diary entries it was clear that there were two modes of interaction at work; one in which the post-holder looks ahead, does the necessary homework, approaches the head and having got the consent to go ahead – does so, but with frequent consultation and encouragement from the head. The other, where the specialist who may, or may not, initiate minor events such as displays of work but whose main function appears to be that of a second pair of hands for the head.

Advice was sought from teachers with posts of responsibility in an *ad hoc* way on many matters, mainly of an ephemeral nature, touching on students on teaching practice, information needed by the head and his deputy. One entry read:

Received news that a secondary English teacher is coming next Wednesday to work in the 4th year with me to see how primary schools develop different aspects of language. (Feel satisfied that the local comp. is more interested (to a limited extent) in the work of primary schools, rather than developing a common schools transfer sheet, for all aspects of English (how ludicrous!).)

5 days later. Informed 4th-year teachers that a secondary teacher from the local comp. would be coming in tomorrow to discuss children with learning difficulties.

Next day. Transpires that the secondary teacher due to come in today is ill. Annoyance felt, because of the rush to finish special reports and arrangements. I had arranged to have all the 4th-year children with reading ages below 90 in a special group, doing selected English activities, for the visiting teacher to see working, to hear read and talk to. The teacher will be coming in on the 19th. Rang local comp. to rearrange time the proposed visit of a member of their staff.

Many recorded entries were of a seasonal nature and were similar in many schools and made it obvious how very energetic primary school teachers are. For example, one diarist recorded:

'Harvest Festival – organization throughout the school. Summer term musical production (3 nights). Summer residential music course – 4 days.

Throughout the year run the following out of school activities: Film Club, Tuesdays band 3.30 – 4.30. Thursday choir 3.30 – 4.15.

Reference was made in the diaries to the local advisory staff. One language specialist recorded a conversation with a member of the Remedial Service on the results of some testing done by the school:

14.7. Discussed with member of Remedial and Language Service the results of Distar Evaluation. All the children showed gains ranging from four to ten months, over a nine month period. We were both disappointed with the inconsistent gains where comprehension was concerned. A general feeling that elements of Distar which ask the children to infer details outside the story tended to handicap these children when they attempted the comprehension questions on the Neale Reading Test. (10 minutes Language Room). Results discussed with head teacher and shown to the two 3rd-year teachers (30 minutes each).

Another recorded that the local music advisor rang with a request that arrangements should be made for the school's violin players to give a demonstration at a talk. In reverse, a music advisor was requested by the teacher responsible for music to bring items into school so that a 'music-display' could be mounted.

Impressions

There are several issues arising from this brief analysis of the diaries, admittedly few, that might usefully be stressed:

1. *Human relationships*   English primary schools are notable for their happy atmosphere. Certainly there was very little tension or drama to be found in the diaries. There was occasional dismay and frustration at the tardiness which attended some requests. There was also resignation:

> . . . this caused the headteacher to tell me off! It seems to me that if I use my initiative I'm liable to displease and if I don't I'm told that certain matters are my concern. You can't win either way.

But in general even when matters possess the potential to upset good relations, they seem to be handled with firmness. For example:

> Confrontation with the Executive Helper who prefers to stay in the 'confinement' of the secretary's office rather than in the curriculum areas working for the teachers as per her timetable. As the lady concerned was supposed to be working for me this morning, I had to chase her up, to find her tearing up old files for the secretary. An argument resulted (which I had anticipated since she relies on teachers not wanting to 'upset the apple cart' to keep her 'easy' job). The result was a worthwhile morning's work on her part . . . Another member of staff witnessed the 'event', so we explained to other staff what had happened to

avoid 'gossip'. I was apprehensive this morning, since I had predicted this problem, but a number of junior staff had complained, so it was essential that some action was seen to be taken by a senior teacher. Final satisfaction that the situation has been corrected.

One week later: ancillary helper is now coming in to me for work at her appointed time, although I have been 'sent to Coventry' by her and the secretary for reproaching her last Thursday. Although this is unpleasant, at least I have the acting Head and the rest of the staff on my side.

No further problems seem to have resulted from this action.

Perhaps the most typical example of how primary schools operate is exemplified by the following:

Discussed things with the Head. She offered to draw out record sheets this morning and this was subsequently done. Later asked one of the staff with a talent for calligraphy to design a Spellball Certificate for winners and runners up of this term's Spellball games in 2nd and 3rd year. We also need certificates for next year. Felt satisfaction that she agreed to do it.

2. *The use of 'specialists'*   There was great disparity in the way that specialists were seen in schools – from the 'role of junior partner to the headteacher' to the 'another pair of hands' role. This can best be seen from the following extracts:

'June 24th. Discussion with Head in his room at lunch time about the introduction of Scottish Primary Maths (SMPG) into the junior department. This has been an ongoing discussion with all members of staff since the New Year. Decision is influenced by the organization of the age groups in the juniors. Decision to introduce the scheme accepted by Head and myself in principle. (A satisfactory encounter.)

Another diarist recalls items such as:

'14.6. Request from Head to remove stage equipment.
No date – set out camping equipment (lunch hour).
Request from Head for sports programme to be completed. (It

was interrupted by dental inspection.)

No date – requested to help staff move a screen.

3. *The lack of help*   The amount of help available to most teachers was scarce. Although ancillary help was mentioned, it was not always at their disposal when most needed. This was evident from the number of menial and routine tasks the teachers performed.

4. *The magnitude of minutiae*   Perhaps the saddest impression of all is the number of items recorded that were trivial, repetitive, but also necessary. Someone had to do them, and that person was a 'specialist'. Often they concerned equipment – putting it out for others to use or returning it for safe keeping. No one would deny that all kinds of tasks have to be undertaken in a primary school, but who does what, how much time these should take up, should perhaps be looked at more carefully if the expertise of every primary teacher is to be made better use of, as the HMI Survey has suggested and teachers with posts of responsibility play their part more fully in the educational life of the school.

In sum

Several things are clear from the evidence of this chapter. For most primary school teachers the expertise to which they would lay claim is that of teaching and it is for this that they accept responsibility *as class teachers*. For the rest, they would lay claim only to informal knowledge which may or may not be of use to their colleagues. When made responsible for such knowledge, they would do their best to make it available in the informal system which is the collegiality of the primary school. Most would seek to avoid imposing such knowledge as *their expertise* on colleagues.

The informal knowledge for which teachers would accept responsibility is the 'particular strengths' of which the 1978 HMI Survey spoke, and headteachers as well as class teachers, believed that the wider use of teachers' particular strengths could be achieved and would have a good effect on primary education. Equally, both heads and teachers appear to take a non-academic stance toward such knowledge.[3] Few heads, when asked about the qualities they would seek when appointing someone to a post of responsibility, mentioned qualities of mind or intellect. Teachers when asked to indicate those functions and activities for which a colleague with a post of responsibility should undertake did not endorse the questionnaire item containing the phrase 'keeping-up-to-date in a particular subject'. Teachers also, and quite evidently, feel uncomfortable with the term *expert*.

There is also a certain inwardness about the evidence. Heads want any training of teachers with posts of responsibility to be school-based. Teachers seek to preserve the informality of the relationships with their colleagues in the give and take of advice. HMIs and LEA advisers are not generally seen as significant sources of expertise. Nor are others outside the school.

However, what cannot be ignored is evidence of the considerable personal dedication of all in the primary school in discharging the multitude of tasks needing to be undertaken, some close to the educational heart of the school, others more peripheral, but still important to the maintenance of a caring community and all in time that has either to be squeezed between the tasks of teaching or, and more likely, donated out of the personal lives of teachers.

It is now to an examination of the essential expertise and central responsibility of the primary school teachers that we turn, in full awareness of the views of primary school teachers and the picture of the way in which a wide variety of responsibilities are discharged. The picture is not always one of organizational efficiency nor of personal satisfaction, but it is of a recognizable reality that is called primary education.

Notes

1. See p.117, 8.40 which recommends that: 'A fuller use of teachers' particular strengths could make a useful contribution to the solution of this problem.'
2. Copies of the original are available from the Department of Curriculum Studies, Faculty of Education, Ring Road North, University of Birmingham, England B15 2TT.
3. See LOISU, C.B.D. and ROSSITER, D. (in press). *The Mathematics Coordinator in the Primary School.* University of Birmingham, Faculty of Education. See also DEPARTMENT OF EDUCATION AND SCIENCE (1982). *Mathematics Counts: The Cockcroft Report.* London: DES.

Part Three

Expertise, Responsibility And Primariness

CHAPTER 4

What Expertise? What Responsibility?

Introduction

The world today is not the same world that saw the publication of the first *Handbook of Suggestions for Teachers*. It is altered in almost every conceivable respect especially in ways which do not make it easy to know with the confidence that clearly informed the writers of the 1905 *Handbook* what to teach young children and with what ends in view. Some degree of uncertainty has always surrounded the question if for no other reason than at bottom education is about the intervening for the *better* in the development of the young. Certainty about what constitutes *better* is seldom, if ever, likely. A high degree of consensus is. Uncertainty remains, however, not only about what constitutes *better* but also about the nature of human development and how it can be influenced. Of the uncertainty which faces the educator Vickers says:

> (It) is compounded today by two factors both unique to our time. The first is new only in degree. The amount of new knowledge, new ways of knowing and new situations needing to be understood has been increasing exponentially for many decades. This correspondingly increases the difficulty of the educator's task of choosing what to teach and of dealing with what is too important to ignore but too recent to understand. The second is new in kind. It becomes increasingly apparent that the future for which educators prepare the next generation will differ from the decades in which they (themselves) have grown up, still more from earlier years, in ways more radical, yet more dependent, on human judgement, than ever before.[1]

It is with an awareness of the nature of the uncertainty which the educator faces that the issue of expertise, responsibility and primariness has to be confronted. With this is mind, what is the primariness that teachers ought to pursue? What expertise will they need and to whom and in what ways should they discharge their responsibilities?

Primariness today and tomorrow

We have seen already in Chapters 1 and 2 how the purposes and content of primary education and the role of the teacher in primary schooling have changed throughout this century. No longer is it sufficient to teach children the elementary skills of reading, writing and arithmetic together with some knowledge of the world in which they live and its culture as well as teach them acceptable attitudes to authority and to each other. We now want what is to be taught, not only taught in broader contexts such as mathematics, language, and science and technology but also for insight and understanding.[2] At times more than this is sought. Children are expected to use language creatively, to explore alternative number systems and propose their own scientific experiments.[3] The range of school work in which children are encouraged to make their own contributions, to question and propose alternatives is nothing less than amazing, at least looked at from the perspective of the early century educator, though even then there were educators who saw just how much children could contribute to their own learning. Today, in many, if not all primary schools, the active participation of children is taken for granted and is an integral part of the educational process.

Behind the use of broader areas of subject matter in the primary school lie apparently the same essential purposes – to make children literate, numerate and sociate – that were held to be valid aims of education at the beginning of the century. In only a limited sense, however is this true. The literacy, numeracy and sociacy that primary education now seeks are much altered. The concept of literacy, for example, which is now pursued recognizes that language enters into every area of learning.[4] Listening, talking, reading and writing, each involving the use of complex language skills, are called for in the learning of almost all that is taught in the primary school. The skills of language are essential to the development of deductive skills, the skills that enter into judgment, and creative skills. Without these skills what children could learn would be very prescribed indeed. 'Literacy', it is claimed, 'is absolutely necessary for the development not only of science but also of history, philosophy, the explicative understanding of literature, and indeed for the explanation of language (including oral speech) itself.'[5]

It is a purpose of primary education to begin the process of making children literate in this expanded sense. It is arguably the most important task of the primary school. Without adequate levels of literacy, there is much that children cannot be taught nor teach themselves. But literacy can only be achieved through the use of subject matter without which the skills of literacy could not be developed to any acceptable level. For subject matter we draw on the world of knowledge, both subjective and objective knowledge; knowledge which is highly codified with agreed signs and symbols, definitions and units of measurement such as we find in mathematics and the sciences as well as knowledge of history, literature, both understanding and making it, and of religions, which in all but a limited degree is not codified knowledge. [6] We talk and write about such knowledge as we see fit using our judgment of the evidence – the facts of history, our experience of reading a novel or a poem and our beliefs about God – as the ingredients of our thinking.

Of importance also is to make children numerate and to do so in a sense which extends beyond the elementary processes of arithmetic. In a world of computers, to be ignorant of the nature of number systems is to possess little or no access to the power of computers to model that enclosed world that is mathematics.

By the same token, not to introduce the young, if only at an elementary level, to the nature of their interrelationships with others, their interaction with social institutions and the roles they may be called on to play, leaves them without beginning insights into the nature of power and authority in society. Without such beginning insights, the basis of sociacy cannot be laid down.

Literacy and subjects

Conventionally subjects are the source of knowledge for teaching even when that teaching is based on broad areas of content and even when quite young children are being taught. The early numbers work of the infant school is derived from mathematics just as early language work is drawn from English or mother-tongue linguistics.

Subjects are often taken as given, as definitive sources of knowledge, of rationality and critical awareness produced by disciplined procedures. Initiation into the knowledge produced by these disciplined procedures and an understanding of the rules governing them are considered by some to lead to the development of the intellect, the mark of an educated person.[7] But this may not be true to the facts. It is more than likely that the disciplined procedures or methods are rules formulated by those who study a subject as a matter of convention and convenience not because they are an integral and necessary part of the subject.

This does not mean that subjects are not useful sources of knowledge. They are. It means that a better way of thinking about each of them may be as an organized 'body of arguments and beliefs about the importance of a certain set of information and skills'[8] rather than as a definitive source of knowledge; better because attention is drawn to the constituent parts of a subject; that is, to:

i)   the information it provides which are the facts of the subject organized in a way that is peculiar to that subject;

ii)   the argument and beliefs which claim that the subject is of particular and peculiar importance in understanding an aspect of reality; arguments which, for example, distinguish physics from chemistry and both from geology and history;

iii)   the skills needed to understand how the basic data of the subject, its facts, are obtained. Such skills are the subject's methods of inquiry.

Better also, because the terms *argument* and *belief* suggest both an openness and a tentativeness. Arguments are open to challenge and beliefs to change. In fact every subject is rooted in a particular form of theory and a way of theorizing and its theory is open to verification and refutation. This is as true of aesthetic subjects as it is of the sciences, though each have very different forms of theory and styles of theorizing. Literacy affords a means of acquiring the information of a subject, of seeing how its facts are put together, of understanding its nature and the view that it provides of an aspect of reality, whether objective or subjective, as well as its ways of inquiring into that reality and testing the truth of its findings. In doing this literacy makes it possible to learn to know *that* and to know *how* about a category of knowledge, enabling one to distinguish fact from theory and to understand a subject's unique rationality.

Subjects can of course be grouped together, for example as science or humanities, as aesthetic and practical subjects. Almost all groupings are in some way flawed but this is unimportant. What is important is that any organization of subjects or selection of subject matter from them for teaching should be made in an awareness of the kind of category of knowledge that the subjects represent and the particular role that any selected subject matter plays in the internal structure of a subject. To select subject matter simply because it will interest the children one is teaching, may well be detrimental to the long-term interests of the children. Subjects and subject matter should be selected because they offer the child an opportunity of developing a variety of important ways of understanding not only the differing realities which he experiences but also of understanding the many realities of scholarship. Doing this develops both the child's mind and his feelings. It may also eventually provide him with the ability to develop arguments about the construction placed on human experience and understanding by others and it will enable him to *seek* the truth.

This may seem a far cry from the concerns of the primary school but it is not. Developing literacy in children is not simply to turn them into young readers, writers and effective talkers. It is to do so with the intention of developing both their minds and their feelings in as wide a variety of desirable ways as is possible.

Subject matter and the teacher

It has been argued that the selection of subject matter is crucial in developing literacy beyond the ability to read, write and talk effectively. The selection and use of subject matter that will play an important part in the progressive development of literacy must be based on a deep, rather than a detailed knowledge of what makes a subject a subject. In particular it will be essential to know how to articulate this knowledge if only because the essence of teaching is the ability to talk others into ways of knowing and understanding at a level which provides a reasonable chance for them to learn. Of course textbooks, teaching materials, television, radio and computer programs may be employed as surrogate for a teacher's talk. However, the principle is the same. If the textbook or computer program is going to teach so that children will have an opportunity to learn rather than reinforce, and even repeat, what they already know, then its subject matter will need to be organized so that it will provide the means whereby the desired learning can take place.[9] In the reality of the classroom, the teacher's talk and textbooks, for example, interact. Even so, the subject matter of each should be doing its job: making it likely that learning will take place.

Knowing the role that a subject or a selection of subject matter can play in the teaching-learning process in the primary school clearly requires a sophisticated expertise on someone's part. Whose? Is it the class teacher's job to know how, for instance, a mathematics scheme or language programme will afford the optimum opportunity for the children in his charge to learn or is it the job of someone in the school who has that depth of knowledge in mathematics or language which will enable him not only to evaluate the scheme but also to explain to the class teacher how, other things being equal, the scheme will do what is required of it? That this kind of subject expertise needs to be available in the primary school must by now be self-evident. It is also undeniably an academic expertise. But it is not proposed here to deal with the question of who should be responsible for it and how that responsibility should be discharged. That will be done later. It is to another area of expertise that we now turn.

Teaching and the teacher

The evidence of the last chapter made it very clear that primary school teachers see their major responsibility and expertise not surprisingly to be that of teaching. It is after all their professional calling. More than that teaching provides them with those personal satisfactions that are its rewards; satisfactions which arise from the positive responses of children to their teaching and from the freedom which most primary school teachers enjoy to organize the work of their classes, albeit within a range of constraints, all in some degree outside their control; constraints arising from the number of children to be taught, the resources available, the wide spread of attitudes toward schooling commonly to be found among children and, above all, the time available to accomplish the tasks of teaching.[10]

What are the tasks that constitute teaching: that expertise for which teachers hold themselves responsible and about which they tend not to wish to seek advice?

It is the purpose of the tasks of teaching, both in their formal and their informal modes to create the conditions that will optimize the chance that the child will learn what the teacher wants him to learn. The use of force is ruled out. The use of rewards and punishments is not. To achieve this end the teacher has to manage a physical context and its resources, organize a group of children, show them what it is they are to learn in a way that will interest them, have them learn it and then ensure by exercise, repetition and further example that it has been learned. What the child learns may be entirely new to them, like learning to read for the first time; or it may be learning to use what has already been learned for another purpose, such as using the ability to write to express oneself or make a statement about one's experience.

This is not by any means all that there is to teaching. The teacher must know what the children in his class are like, the stage of intellectual and emotional development they are at as well as understand how children learn concepts, skills, attitudes and acceptable forms of social and moral behaviour. This 'professional knowledge' is crucial to the effective discharge of the tasks of teaching which are intended to serve a variety of desirable, frequently interdependent ends. The teaching of one form of knowledge will, for example, impinge on other forms of knowledge, and as teaching is taking place, attitudes to school work, to learning and being taught, to loving some and hating other lessons and seeing some topics as easy and others as difficult are being learned. Teaching must recognize this and use whatever means will work to ensure that its effects are mainly positive.

How the tasks of teaching are articulated is a question of style and teaching style is not only a matter of a teacher's beliefs about his role and that of his pupils but also a question of the extent to which a teacher is free to teach as he wishes.[11] Freedom in this respect is rarely absolute nor ever completely constrained. It may have to accommodate itself to the policy of the school, the local authority, and with increasing insistence, central government, to the generally held views of colleagues and to the expectations of parents.

Teachers' beliefs, sometimes referred to as their philosophy or ideology of education, are a critical component of their teaching style, determining in large measure the way they talk about education (their rhetoric) and the way they account for what happens during the teaching process and what makes it work and to a lesser, though uncertain extent, how they conduct their teaching. Teachers' beliefs will include views about childhood as, for example, a state of being valid in itself or a stage on the way toward adulthood and full membership of society, together with views about society, whether it is a 'good' or 'bad' place, is or is not capable of improvement and the part education is expected to play in conserving or changing, reproducing or reforming its economic, political and social systems.[12]

Teachers' beliefs will vary not only in relation to their perceptions of the role of education in society, the nature of childhood and their preferred teaching style but most significantly, in relation to the ages, and cultural and social background of the children whom they teach. The ages of the children whom they teach will particularly effect the educational objectives considered to be appropriate, and not just simply appropriate but also in large measure achievable. Teachers of five-year-olds teach them the beginnings of much: reading, writing and number work. They also teach them the beginning basics of being a person in public as well as school-appropriate behaviour; in essence the acceptance of school and classroom routines.

Teachers of ten-year-olds will, in general, take it for granted that the basics have been taught, though they may well continue to reinforce them, and aim their teaching at more complex intellectual and social objectives, at, for example, problem-solving in mathematics and at developing an understanding of differing kinds of social and moral conduct.[13]

Teachers in schools serving inner city catchment areas will tend to emphasize the basic skills of conventional literacy, especially the fundamentals of reading, writing and mathematics for longer and more didactically than teachers in schools serving suburban catchment areas.[14]

Teachers and the technology of teaching

The tasks of teaching, as we have seen, are circumscribed by many factors, some beyond the control of teachers, such as the social backgrounds of the children they have to teach. Some are in large measure within the control of teachers. How, for example, they manage the routines and regularities of the classroom in which they teach. One factor, already touched on, within the control of the teacher, is the know-how or technology of teaching, the knowledge and tools on which teachers may draw to accomplish the tasks of teaching.

We have already made it clear (p.110) what are the tasks of the teacher (or those substitutes for them, textbooks, radio, television and computer programmes) that are at the heart of teaching. All we need do here is to point to them as *the* most important aspect of the technology of teaching. How a teacher explains what is to be learned, instances and clarifies it are critical to effective teaching, so is the use of the voice, the success with which it gains and sustains attention, directs activities, ensures order and the effective management of the classroom.

In addition, some of the skills of the actor are called for, though the teacher must be his own director and producer as well as writing, at least in his head and as he goes along, his own scripts. Gesture, exaggeration, eye contact, pitch and tenor of voice, use of the space of the classroom, its stage, empathy with the audience and, at times, use of that kind of guile which makes a performance memorable.[15]

The teacher then, his voice, manner, range of roles, talent for producing scripts, his own or others, that will not only hold his audience but also persuade them to undertake sometimes difficult and at times repetitive tasks, is the most important element in his technology. He is himself the larger part of the know-how of teaching.

Teachers also need to know how to employ a range of physical resources for specific purposes: visual and aural aids, the blackboard, space in the classroom and around the school, both inside and out, and of course curriculum materials including text and many other types of books. More recently, and not yet to be found in every primary school classroom, there is both the micro-computer and electronic teaching devices which teachers need to know how to use. Even so, the physical technology of teaching is not extensive, though its effective use in teaching may require sophisticated articulation.

Integral to the know-how of teaching is the knowledge teachers need to draw on in order to teach effectively, the knowledge of children, how they learn to think and feel, what motivates them, how the social setting of school and classroom create good or poor contexts for learning and the effects of home background on attitudes to schooling. The knowledge is psychological and sociological, not in an academic or specialist sense but as the ongoing knowledge of practitioners.[16] As is the case with many non-technical, human technologies, teachers learn to improve their practices largely by trial and error and each teacher is his own judge of what works. Teachers learn a great deal at the margin, about new language schemes, for example, or about the findings of recent surveys in primary education and about new developments in understanding the psychology of childhood at conferences and on courses, but they learn little that is new that they will use that is central to their role or their own teaching, unless it is to change from one way of organizing teaching to another, from class teaching, say, to teaching based on groups. It is also the case that teachers tend to accord a secondary position to officially designated sources of help, local authority advisers and HMIs, and will more readily accept help from colleagues if it is about *what* rather than the *how* of teaching.[17]

Finally, knowledge of *what* to teach, whether it is essential to the development of skills, the acquisition of information or attitudes, as was argued earlier in this chapter (p.109), is basic to the technology of teaching. Without a content teaching is not simply hollow, it is non-existent. Much of the *what* of teaching in the primary school is concerned to develop children's minds, to give them skills which will enable them to think not only increasingly for themselves but also about those ways of organizing human experience which have engaged the attention of human beings for generations and which form part of our culture. To know the *what* of teaching is to understand its theoretical foundations, to be aware of the structural principles which hold it together. This is essential knowledge for teaching if for no other reason than that these principles show how the information of a category of knowledge is held in place. Without such knowledge, much teaching will verge on the vacuous. Children may be informed but lack the ability to give more than a superficial meaning to what they know.

It is on the theory or theories of knowledge that the knowledge of *what* to teach depends.[18] Such a theory or theories are not fixed and final. They are frequently a matter of contention among philosophers, scientists, historians, in linguistics and between geographers. This does not stop scientists creating new understandings of the natural world nor historians writing their histories. By the same token, it should not stop teachers, even of very young children, seeking to be clear in their own minds what principles inform the knowledge they employ. This is true whether environmental studies rather than history or geography is being taught. In fact much that is taught in primary school will not be formal subject matter. Nevertheless, it should have a meaning based on the organized bodies of argument that constitute such subject matter.

That teaching seems to many to be a commonsense activity, even to its practitioners, is understandable. That it is *not* is abundantly clear once its processes and technology are examined. It is claimed with justification that teaching

. . . has been permitted to remain evanescent; there is no equivalent to the recording found in surgical cases, law cases, and physical models of engineering and architectural achievement. Such records, coupled with commentaries and critiques of highly trained scholars, allow new generations to pick up where earlier ones left off.

Attempts have been made to explain teaching in psychological terms focussing more on how children learn than on how teaching succeeds.[19] The sociology of teaching (even educating) is widely studied by beginning teachers, and by experienced teachers on advanced courses, but with few exceptions it too fails to focus on the commonplaces of teaching, on its practices and persisting regularities. Teachers themselves rarely write critically about what they do though occasionally they write anecdotally with insight.[20]

Why teaching remains a commonsense activity rather than a technically informed process is difficult to say. The endemic uncertainties surrounding education about what to teach, how to teach it and with what ends in view may be one reason. Another may be that objective documentation of what teachers daily do in their classrooms may show a routinization which ill fits the sometimes exalted claims made for the teacher's calling. However, a more than likely reason is that much, if not all, teaching in the primary school is insulated behind the classroom door and takes place in the personal domain of the individual teacher. This insulation creates not simply occupational independence, teachers learn early to fend for themselves, but also limits the information about what is happening to that selected by the teacher himself. It may not be the best information out of which to construct an understanding of how teaching succeeds and where it fails. On the other hand, hundreds of studies based on direct and independent observation of teaching have failed to do more than offer a limited insight into what makes teaching effective.[21] Other studies based on teaching as a human not a technical process offer a better promise but are unlikely to approach the latent understanding possessed by generations of teachers.[22]

The wider context

Most primary school teachers will spend the greater part of their working lives in their own classrooms, with their own children, reinforcing a personality preferred style of teaching, generally a traditional one and enjoying the satisfactions of teaching young children. Even so, they will be aware of the main features of the society whose children they school, its moral, economic and social character. The teachers will know that the life of childhood outside the school is very different from that of their own childhood. In particular it is lived on the threshold of the electronic and vocal whose symbols are the TV, the Walkman, the cassette, the disc and the rock concert. The childhood of today cannot fail to be touched by the language of the pop song and the commercial. This new literacy is not only intensely oral it is also intensely immediate. Most often it is seen as a corruption of language when in fact it is the language of today's popular art. As such it has had its counterpart at other times, in other ages and ' . . . like the artistic output of any generation, most of it is trite, but its successes are dazzling'.[23] It is at times vigorous, vital and witty. It is difficult to ignore and so far, impossible to incorporate into education. But it should teach one thing: that it will become part of the literacy of most children whether we like it or not.

Contemporary childhood will also be touched by the moral, social and political attitudes of today and what they may presage for tomorrow. We live in a largely secular, market-dominated society which uses education to produce people with the skills necessary to service its needs, the fundamental of which is the need to maximize economic and technological growth. The desire to develop in everyone critical awareness and interpretive insight, the hallmarks of a liberal education is largely gone.[24] Moreover, in a world of personality, the development of character qualities through education is seldom discussed.

In political life there is cynicism about the use of power both on the part of politicians and the electorate. Political life is no longer seen as an honourable calling, more a necessary evil. Politicians must respond more to today's crises than the long-term interests of a country. All is imminent, of the here and now. This is not to condemn political life in the modern democracy. Merely to say that public life in the latter part of the twentieth century is different in character from previous centuries.[25]

Public life for which schools prepare children is altered in other and more fundamental respects. It has been changed by the combined effects of capitalism and secularism on our consciousness; on our awareness of ourselves and others. There has been 'an erosion of belief in experience external to the self'. Narcissism*, the attempt to comprehend reality through images of the self, has replaced it.[26] Intimate feelings have become a measure of the meaning of social reality. The immediate consequence of this in public life has been the erosion of interest in the life of the city and the growth of interest in the neighbourhood, in the local community. Some describe this shift as 'retribalization', others as 'ghettoization'. Whichever is the more apt, there can be little doubt that the modern city is in crisis.[27]

Not only has public life altered but so has the nature of work. Automation and robotization are but two aspects of this. These processes have taken labour out of work. They have also deskilled some and reskilled others. But perhaps the most important change has been the extent to which work has come increasingly to be seen

---

*The story of Narcissus is of the boy so fascinated by the reflection of himself in a pool that, despite warnings of danger, he leans over to caress it and falls into the pool and drowns.

as a matter of technique; as a technical rather than a human enterprise. As such work loses its capacity to form character; its moral connections with the practical side of life is severed.

Changes in the nature of work, public and political life, in the life of childhood and in human consciousness, all have implications for the moral enterprise that is education: for how we intervene for the better in the development of children. It is against such a backdrop that the issue of the expertise and responsibility of the primary school teacher needs to be examined and the nature of the primariness restated. It has to be done in the full awareness that the primary school is *in* society. Its own current dilemmas are not unrelated to the contemporary problems of society. Nevertheless, the education which primary schools provide must attempt to equip the child for the society of tomorrow.

Expertise, responsibility and primariness

By now it must be clear that the expertise on which the primary school teacher needs to draw is twofold. It is knowledge about knowledge, the understanding of the forms of argument and belief from which any body of knowledge is compiled *and* knowledge of teaching, its practical arts and essential insights. The first is intellectual. It is the mind's understanding of the *what* of teaching. The second is the practical appreciation of the *how* of teaching. For the primary school the achievement of a high level of literacy is its functional goal. Literacy at the end of primary schooling should achieve a threshold capacity for listening, talking, reading and writing across a variety of knowledge codes: in mathematics, science, history, geography, language and literature or within subject groupings. What primary school teachers must come to terms with is that

> the uses of literacy have greatly expanded in this century. It becomes increasingly costly to accept the unjustified assumption that a collection of literary or basic skills will transfer too to these many different literary uses.[28]

Not only must literacy in its much expanded sense become the stock in trade of primary education but it must increasingly be recognized as essential to the development of thresholds of thought, feeling and action in many subject areas, not only of intellectual endeavour but also of social and moral insight in children. This view of literacy includes understanding story and play both of which are of great importance in the education of all children, especially of the very young. Child play which involves rules, teaches self-distance. The rules enable children to objectify action: ' . . . to put it at a distance and change it qualitatively.'[29] Story allows experience to be accounted for in both the *story* and the *real* world.[30]

Through a reappraisal of the role and nature of literacy primary education can promise enhanced levels of achievement but only if teachers can draw either individually or collegially on improved stocks of knowledge and a sound appreciation of what makes teaching effective in both its formal and informal mode.

Who then should be responsible for ensuring that there are improved stocks of knowledge for teachers to draw upon and an enhanced and a growing appreciation of what makes teaching effective? Many, if not most, primary schools cannot turn to specialist teaching even for upper juniors as a means of enhancing the stock of knowledge on which they can draw. They do not have sufficient staff. Most will need either to increasingly adapt posts of responsibility for this purpose or, and more radically, accept the responsibility as a collegial one. This last, if it is to be effective, will require both changes in the power structure within the school and a hard-headed approach to the quality of discussion. In short, professional rather than personal criteria will need to inform judgment and decision about *what* to teach, its structure and sequencing. There will be less scope for choice by individual teachers but more participation in decision-making.

Much the same could apply to making teaching increasingly effective but would be more difficult to achieve. That was the message of Chapter 3. Teaching is the individual teacher's stock in trade. It is the essence of his professional standing which is rooted in practical knowledge shaped by experience. Teachers will only change how they teach if they are reasonably certain that the new approach will work for them. Like people in other professions, they will not readily risk damage to their reputations. But unlike people in other professions, teachers have access only to a limited and barely growing pool of professional knowledge. Moreover, much of this knowledge is ideologically coloured if not contaminated, marked as 'traditional' or 'progressive', teacher or pupil-centred and is most frequently used to justify or denounce one or other educational fashion. It would also appear that teachers as a profession do not look to past achievements as evidence of their professional capabilities. It has even been asserted that teachers engage in the : ' . . . repetitive discrediting of the past.'[31]

Whatever is the case, it is clear that if the primary school teacher is not to be cast increasingly in the role of trainer, rather than educator, teaching to prescribed objectives, using approved materials and with his efforts subject to approved measures of performance, he will need to tackle the question of what makes teaching effective with far greater rigour and determination than has been evidenced in the past. The much cherished autonomy of the primary school teacher is not part of the natural order of things. It is a condition which has grown out of the past; a past which was less demanding of educational achievement over a less extensive range of understandings than the present. It now matters what professional response the primary school teacher makes to these changed educational expectations.

Even more is at stake than the potential bureaucraticization of teaching.[32] What is at stake is the very education of children themselves in a world in which almost every possible uncertainty is endemic. The economic, social, political and moral systems of society are less stable now than at any time for many generations.[33] Without professional autonomy the teacher is in a poor position to argue for what is for the best in the development of the children whom he teaches. What must be noted is that teaching is part of the moral enterprise of education. The more it approximates to training the less moral authority it has. But the moral authority of teaching is tied to the extent to which *in practice* teaching can achieve what is expected of it, even when these expectations are for higher attainment over a wider area of subject matter. On the degree to which teaching rises to the task confronting it, will depend its moral authority.

Today the moral authority of teaching may best be exercised in somewhat conservative terms. Neither the untrammelled child-centred education of the Plowden variety nor the equally procrustean teacher-centred education of the Black Papers is warranted. They both belong to a vigorous educational past and as such have much to teach. Teachers should seek to learn their lessons: when to let children follow their own interests and when to explain to them how best to acquire a skill or an understanding. Teaching will also need to become a more critically reflective enterprise and less a matter of personal opinion. Increasingly its wisdom will need to become less received and more dispassionate; its questioning more rigorous, especially of how teaching in some schools succeeds despite the same array of constraints which limit the achievement of other schools. No more is being suggested than that teachers contribute to their own professional knowledge. To do this many teachers' fear of expertise may need to be overcome.

The issue of generalist, class teacher or specialist subject teacher is partly a question of how best to raise levels of achievement in primary education. As such it is a technical question. It is also a question of how best the teacher may exercise his moral authority. What goes on in the primary school and its classroom influences the value, both instrumental and ethical, that children place on what they learn. It affects their consciousness. It is, therefore, on both levels that the question needs to be asked and answered, and evaluated at least so long as the teacher is the free moral agent that he is.

The primariness that is pursued in primary schools is not unrelated to both the moral and technical concerns of society. It remains to do with literacy, again in both its technical and moral aspects but across a broader spectrum than at previous times. The responsibility of the primary school teacher is to understand the nature of primariness *as it is becoming,* to articulate this both for themselves and for society. It is through their expertise that it has to be taught. This expertise has both a knowledge and a teaching component. An understanding of both is critical to effective teaching. Equally, the teacher needs to understand the good he seeks to do through his engagement in primary education. His obligations as an educator demand this. His ability to discharge this obligation requires a degree of professional autonomy which in turn rests on his ability through the expertise of teaching to satisfy the expectations society holds for primary education.

The primary school teacher's responsibility and expertise both individually and collegially are interrelated. How best these are to be discharged under changed and changing circumstances must become a matter of urgent professional inquiry to which this book is but a contribution. The larger part is yet to be undertaken. Meantime there are steps that can be taken.

Some ways ahead

A first and priority step, which is very difficult to take, is to attempt to understand better the problem. It is a step made more difficult by the fact that many of the current initiatives to improve standards in the primary school serve to obscure the nature of the problem. The Department of Education's series *Curriculum Matters* is a case in point. They assert common educational ground where in fact little exists that is not empty of substantive meaning. What does it mean: 'to help pupils use language and number effectively,'[33] which is not empty? Were it not trite, it would need to argue what view of the nature of language and number was to be adopted if one was to *know how* to help, and what were to be the criteria of effectiveness.

The same is true of the plea to establish agreed objectives for the components of the curriculum. Where the enhanced quality of educational life is critical for improvement of standards, there would seem little point in presuming what could or should be achieved in terms of performance criteria, especially as those criteria focus only on the behaviour of those who are taught and not on the qualities of mind and professional capability of those who teach. It was the Plowden Report that seized the point: 'On the teachers, on their skills and good will, far more than on organization or on building, the future of education depends', adding: 'There is little hope that children will come to an appreciation of order and beauty either in nature or what is man-made, unless these qualities are enjoyed by their teachers and exemplified in the schools.'[34] Order and beauty are enjoyed only to the degree to which they are understood. Understanding means quite literally both seeing on what something stands, its essential nature and seeing the presence of that essential nature as it is, and has been, presented to human experience.

The problem to be understood then, is that improved standards in primary education, as opposed to improved performance, depends as much if not more, on the better understanding by teachers of what they teach, its essential qualities, as on their greater efforts to teach better what they already do. Probably more so.

A second step is to cast the idea of specialist teaching in the primary school not in terms of specialist *subject* teachers but in terms of teachers with a *special* understanding of those modes of thought, feeling (or love of) and rationality (or order) which make for those broad areas of understanding through which we organize human experience – language, science, including mathematics, technology and not forgetting environmental studies, the humanities and the arts – in both their using and their productive or creative sides.[35] Such teachers could make their special understanding available to their colleagues in a variety of ways: through talking about how they see it, illustrating it, in teaching materials and specimen lessons; in critically appraising textbooks, curriculum project materials and HMI and DES recommendations.

Together with a teacher's special understanding has to go the readiness to assert this knowledge. Teachers may need training in this.[36] Many years of deferring to the superior knowledge of others coupled with an ambivalence toward scholarship does not equip teachers to adopt an authoritative view of their own professional knowledge, nor provide the assurance that they can develop an adequate theory of knowledge to inform their teaching. And it is nothing less that is needed.[37]

Clearly, neither greater confidence nor the development of special knowledge will be easy to secure but some pioneering work has been done which suggests a possible strategy: teacher self-researching. Stenhouse was the pioneer.[38] The basis of the strategy arises from the frequently noticed fact, as Schon puts it:

> When intuitive, spontaneous performance, yields nothing more than the result expected of it, then we tend *not* to think about it. But when intuitive performance leads to surprises, pleasing and promising or unwanted, we may respond by reflecting-in-action.[39]

As Rudduck says it is for the teacher to be 'sensitive to surprise and stalwart enough in resisting the relentless pressure of the classroom to take advantage of it'.[40]

Self-researching has, however, to go further than 'reflecting-in-action'. It has to be experimental as well, changing qualitatively that most critical of variables in the teaching-learning process, the substance of what one is teaching and desires pupils to learn and understand, and then assessing the extent to which they have understood it. Such assessment has to be more than mere testing. It has to be that form of criticism which leads to: ' . . . the re-education of perception';[41] to interpretation and appraisal; to seeing how changing the texture of one's teaching has or has not improved its quality. Eisner[42] has written widely on this. At heart educational criticism requires nothing less than that a teacher talk to himself about the qualities of the educational life of the classroom that he is attempting to enhance.

Talking about quality is not easy especially to oneself.[43] To do so well, even with others, requires experience and sensitivity, but above all the command of an appropriate language. Teachers do not talk about what they do in the language of psychology or sociology. They use ordinary language in a rather special way. It is this every day language and the way it is used by teachers that will have to be called into play and refined so that it increasingly reveals the educational qualities which the teacher seeks to identify.

What is being urged here is that teachers more consciously represent to themselves actions of their teaching and its content in ways luminous for a better understanding of what those actions (and their content) result in and how they may be qualitatively improved.

Curriculum courses might profitably take account of the need teachers have to understand better the content of their teaching, and for developing appreciative insights into their teaching. In achieving this such courses will need to reflect the essential preoccupations of the teacher with his teaching and use illustrative material drawn from the classroom and be alert to its realities.

In conclusion

Improving the stock of special knowledge available to the primary school teacher and the qualities of teaching deployed in the school are central to the improvement of the standards in primary eduction. But there are severe constraints to be overcome. The limited time primary school teachers have for planning reflection and appreciative judgment[44] is a severe constraint. So may be the persisting regularities of primary education; those taken-for-granted routines with which the day begins, lessons and activities start and the customary vocabulary of the teacher as he enacts what he believes teaching entails.

For some primary schools a significant constraint may arise from the home and cultural background of the children whom they have to teach. Such constraints have long been known about, if imperfectly understood, and primary schools adapt themselves to them mostly by trial and error, a form of approximation management through which uncertainties are coped with in many areas of practical affairs.[45]

Finally, it has to be recognized that primary schools have obligations in addition to the central one of teaching young children. The need to exercise pastoral responsibility, for example, and sometimes to leaven the tasks of learning with special occasions. Primary schools have also to spend time representing themselves to parents and to the local community, not always an easy task.

With such a constellation of constraints to overcome and obligations to discharge, it is not surprising that time to think about teaching is scarce. It is just because it is scarce that it should be used efficiently and applied to how to improve the quality of life lived in the classroom of the primary school not only for the children, but also, and as importantly, for teachers. It has been the message of this book that the critical expertise of the primary school teacher resides largely in himself. It is his responsibility to give to it those qualities that will from time to time, raise the level of primary education. If there was ever a time for such a leap forward, that time is now.

At the outset of this book the question was asked, 'How much a curriculum generalist and how much a subject specialist should a primary school teacher be?' It has been answered in part but only tentatively. What it is hoped is clear by now is that every primary school teacher should be a specialist at teaching and know clearly what it constitutes to be in command of such special technical knowledge. Part of this knowledge will be to admit a degree of uncertainty about how to improve it, if only because the ends which teaching serves are themselves uncertain and subject to change.

As to the primary school teacher being a subject specialist, there can be no doubt, or so it has been argued, that he will need to be able to draw on specialist knowledge and knowledge of an increasingly sophisticated nature as time goes on. How such knowledge is to be made available to him is a practical matter still in large measure to be worked out. It is, however, the balance of the evidence from Part Two that there is a marked professional preference that the primary school teacher should for the most part remain a curriculum generalist. It is a professional preference yet to be tested against the emerging primariness of the last decade and a half of the twentieth century.

References and notes

1. VICKERS, G. (1973). 'Educational criteria for times of change,' *Journal of Curriculum Studies*, **5**, 1, 13-24.
2. To some extent this is the burden of the HMI Primary School Survey, see ALEXANDER, R. (1984) *Primary Teaching*. London: Holt Rinehart & Winston. Alexander suggests that science will become the third basic.
3. RICHARDS, C. and HOLFORD, D. (eds) (1983). *The Teaching of Primary Science: Policy and Practice*. Lewes: Falmer Press.
4. DECASTELL, S., LUKE, A. and EGAN, K. (eds) (1985). *Literacy, Schooling and Society*. Cambridge: University of Cambridge Press. Also see Steiner G. (1971) Future Literacies from *In Bluebeard's Castle* in *George Steiner: a Reader*. Harmondsworth, Penguin.
5. ONG, W.J. (1982) *Orality and Literacy; the Technologising of the Word*. London: Methuen.
6. THOMPSON, J. (1969). 'Truth strategies and university organisation,' *Educational Administration Quarterly*, **5**, 2, 4-25.
7. This is essentially the argument made by such philosophers of education as R.S. Peters and Paul Hirst. The latter's essay 'Education Theory' published in TIBBLE, J.W. (1966). *The Study of Education*, London, Routledge and Kegan Paul is a classic statement of the case.
8. For a discussion on this point, see FEINBERG, W. (1983). *Understanding Education*. Cambridge: Cambridge University Press.
9. See GARLAND, R. (ed) (1982). *Microcomputers and Children in the Primary Schools*. Lewes: Falmer Press.
10. Useful studies of constraints are to be found in TAYLOR, P.H., REID, W.A., HOLLEY, B.J. and EXON,G. (1974). *Purpose, Power and Constraint in the Primary School Curriculum*. London: Macmillan Educational and TAYLOR, P.H. (ed) (1975). *Aims, Influence and Change in the Primary School Curriculum*. Windsor: NFER Publishing Co.
11. Teaching style has been the subject of several studies. Two important and relevant ones are BENNETT, S.N. *et al.* (1976). *Teaching Styles and Pupils' Progress*. London: Open Books and POWELL, J. (1985). *The Teacher's Craft*. Edinburgh: Scottish Council for Educational Research.
12. For some correlates of teacher's ideologies see Chapter 8, 'The Teacher's Role' in ASHTON, P., KNEEN, P., DAVIES, F. and HOLLEY, B.J. (1975). *The Aims of Primary Education*. London: Macmillan Educational.

13. For evidence on this point see TAYLOR, P.H. and HOLLEY, B.J. 'A Study of the Emphasis given by Teachers of Different Age Groups to Aims in Primary Education.' In: TAYLOR, P.H. (ed) (1975). *Aims, Influence and Change in Primary Education.* Windsor: NFER-NELSON.

14. The first evidence of this was reported in WISEMAN, S. (1963). *Education and Environment.* Manchester: Manchester University Press.

15. Rex Oram has been exploring a dramaturgical model of teaching, a theory of which he outlines in his paper ORAM, R. (1978). 'An action frame of reference as a register for curriculum discourse,' *Journal of Curriculum Studies*, **10**, 2, 135-49.

16. An interesting analogue with how the teacher learns can be made with how general practitioners learn as opposed to physicians and surgeons. See HAGE, J. (1974). *Communication and Organisational Control.* London: John Wiley.

17. For evidence of this, see PRIMARY SCHOOLS RESEARCH AND DEVELOPMENT GROUP (1978). *Primary School Teachers' Attitudes to Issues Raised in the Great Debate.* Birmingham: Teaching Research Unit.

18. This is clearly evident from even a cursory examination of any 'philosophy of education' from Plato to the present. For a useful commentary see MATTHEW, M.R. (1980). *Marxist Theory of Schooling.* Brighton: Harvester Press.

19. LORTIE, D. (1975). *Schoolteacher.* London: University of Chicago Press.

20. A good example was Edward Blishen's *Roaring Boys*, published in 1955.

21. See the analysis of several hundred studies in ROSENSHINE, B. (1971). *Teaching Behaviours and Student Achievement.* Windsor: NFER-NELSON.

22. A new generation of researchers offer promise here. A recent example is HARTLEY, D. (1985). *Understanding the Primary School.* London: Croom Helm.

23. See PATTISON, R. (1982). *On Literacy; The Politics of the Word from Homer to the Age of Rock.* Oxford: Oxford University Press. Pattison is of the opinion that ways can be found to include within the language education of the young what he calls 'the nascent literacy of the people'.

24. See the claims of Ruth Jonathan in (1983) 'The manpower service model of education,' *Cambridge Journal of Education*, **13**, 2 and (1985) 'Education, philosophy of education and context,' *Journal of Philosophy of Education*, **19**, 1, 13-25. Also see FEINBERG, W. (1975). *Reason and Rhetoric.* London: John Wiley and RAVITCH, D. (1983). *The Troubled Crusade.* New York: Basic Books.

25. LASCH, C (1984). *The Minimal Self: Psychic Survival in Troubled Times.* London: Picador, and RICHARD SENNETT (1979) who makes much the same argument in *The Decline of Public Man*, Cambridge, Cambridge University Press.

26. For an excellent analysis see SENNETT, R. (1970). *The Uses of Disorder: Personal Identity and City Life.* New York: Vintage Books.

27. HARSTE, J.C. and MIKULECKY, L.J. 'The Context of Literacy in Our Society'. In: PURVES, A.C. and NILES, O. (1984). 'Becoming Readers in a Complex Society,' *83rd Yearbook Part 1 of National Society for the Study of Education:* Chicago: University Press.

28. See Sennett *op. cit. sup.* especially Chapter 14, 313-336. The Actor Deprived of his Art.

29. See WADE, B. (1984). *Story at Home and School.* Birmingham: Educational Review Occasional Publications.

30. See LORTIE, D.C. (1975). *Schoolteacher.* Chicago: University of Chicago Press.

31. It was clear from the study noted above (n.17) that the more probable of two possible future scenarios for primary school teachers involved increasing bureaucratization.

32. See BERMAN, M. (1982). *All that is Solid Melts into the Air: the Experience of Modernity.* New York: Simon and Shuster. Much of the uncertainty of the modern world was foreseen by the nineteenth century philosopher Nietzsche and even earlier by the poet William Blake.

33. DEPARTMENT OF EDUCATION AND SCIENCE (1985). *The Curriculum from 5 to 16: Curriculum Matters 2.* London: HMSO.

34. CENTRAL ADVISORY COUNCIL FOR EDUCATION vol. 1 (1967). *Children and their Primary Schools.* The Plowden Report. London: HMSO.

35. Here one needs to make the distinction that Whitehead made between inert and living knowledge in WHITEHEAD, A.N. (1929). *Aims of Education.* London: William Northgate.

36. KELLEY, C. (1979). *Assertion Training: a facilitator's guide.* London/ New York: University Associates.

37. An interesting exploration of this point is to be found in HARTNETT and NAISH 'Toward a Sociology of Educational Belief.' In: HARTNETT, A. (Ed) (1982). *The Social Sciences in Educational Studies.* London: Heinemann. See also WARNOCK, M. (1977). *Schools of Thought.* London: Faber and Faber; PRING, R. (1976). *Knowledge and Schooling.* London: Open Books.

38. See, for example, STENHOUSE, L. (1984). 'Artistry and Teaching: the Teacher as the Focus of Research and Development.' In: HOPKINS, D. and WIDEEN, M. (eds) *Alternative Perspectives on School Improvement.* Lewes: Falmer Press.

39. SCHON, D.A. (1983). *The Reflective Practitioner.* New York: Basic Books.

40. RUDDUCK, J. (1985). 'Teacher research and research based teacher education', *Journal of Education for Teaching,* **11**, 3, 281-9.

41. VICKERS, G. (1970). *Value Systems and the Social Process.* Harmondsworth: Penguin Books.

42. See EISNER, E. (1979). *The Educational Imagination.* London: Collier Macmillan.

43. For an interesting discussion of 'quality' see PIRSIG, R. (1976). *Zen and*

the Art of Motor-Cycle Maintenance. London: Corgi Books.
44. For an exposition of 'appreciative judgement' see VICKERS, G. (1967). *The Art of Judgement.* London: Chapman Hall.
45. It is the theory of practices rather than theory as such, that is needed in education, and there is some evidence that teachers know this though not how to develop such a theory. See for example, TAYLOR, P.H. (1973). 'A limited empirical study of the attitudes of serving teachers to educational theory,' *Research in Education,* 10 November, 1-12.

Appendices

APPENDIX 1a

Interview Schedule – Teacher With A Post Of Responsibility

Part A

1. Male/female
2. Teaching qualifications
3. How long have you been teaching?
4. What is your area of responsibility?
5. Is there a written job description for your post of responsibility? If so, does it accurately describe what you do?
6. How is your role influenced by: a) your head? b) your local authority inspectors or advisers? c) published teachers' guides? d) relevant in-service courses, both full and part time?
7. Are you able, as a teacher with a post of responsibility, to influence other teachers in your school? If so, which teachers?
8. In terms of your area of responsibility, how is advice and help sought and given, by whom? Is this valuable, and are the procedures satisfactory?

Part B

1. Is the term 'teacher expert' appropriate for people with posts of special responsibility for curriculum areas?
2. To what extent is teacher expertise in particular curriculum areas desirable in the primary school today?
3. In which curriculum areas is teacher expertise required? Why those areas and how should it be made available?
4. How is it possible to develop the *role* of the teacher expert?
5. Can the professional expertise of primary school teachers be improved?
    If so, how do you think this can be achieved?

APPENDIX 1b

Interview Schedule – Teacher

Part A

1. Male/female
2. Teaching qualifications
3. How long have you been teaching
4. a) Are there teachers with special posts of responsibility in your school?
   b) Are any of these for particular curriculum areas?
   If so, please say which.
5. If Yes to 4 a), does the system work?
6. What is the value of having posts of responsibility?
7. Can the role of the post-holder be improved?
8. If so, how?
9. Do teachers with posts of responsibility influence other teachers in your school?
10. In your experience, how is advice and help given – by whom and under what circumstances?

Part B

1. How do you view the *idea* of the 'teacher expert' in particular curriculum areas?
2. In which curriculum areas is teacher expertise required?
   Why those areas, and how should it be made available?
3. Can the professional expertise of primary school teachers be improved?
   How do you think this can be achieved?

APPENDIX 2

Headteachers' Questionnaire

The purpose of this questionnaire is to seek your views on the use of scale posts and the idea of wider use of teacher expertise than at present.

There is space at the end of the questionnaire for any general comments which you may wish to make.

Section 1

1:1 How long have you been the head of your present school?

years _____

1:2 Have you previously been a head?

Yes

No

If 'yes', for how many years?

years _____

1:3 Which of the following qualifications do you possess?

Teachers' certificate

BEd

Postgraduate certificate

BA or BSc

MEd

Advanced qualification in education

Section 2

2:1 To which of the following areas of responsibility
are scale posts allocated in your school?
a) Teaching and curriculum responsibilities (e.g.
language work, games etc.)
b) Resource responsibilities (e.g. organizing
library, reprographic responsibilities etc.)
c) Welfare and liaison responsibilities (e.g.
pastoral care, liaison with other schools or
institutions etc.)
d) Administrative and organizing responsibilities
(e.g. organizing a school event, administrative
duties relating to the school office etc.)
e) Other (please specify)

2:2 Where scale posts are for teaching and curriculum
responsibilities, to which of the following curriculum areas are
they allocated, and for what purpose? Please indicate by
placing a tick in the appropriate place. If more than one post
is allocated to a particular area will you please indicate the
fact.

Curriculum area	Preparing schemes of work	Advising on teaching methods	Advising on methods of assessment	Managing resources
Mathematics				
Science				
History, Geog. Soc. studies				
Religious ed.				
Music				
Language & reading skills				
Art & craft				
Environmental studies & topic work				
PE & games				

2:3 What criteria would you look for in appointing a post-holder with responsibility for an area of curriculum and teaching? For example, would you look for long service to the school – someone with a compatible philosophy of education – a person who had good relations with colleagues – someone eager to change educational practices – or a person who gets on well with parents? *Please indicate below*, in note form if you wish, the criteria you would employ:

_____

_____

_____

_____

_____

_____

_____

_____

2:4 How much time in school do you expect post-holders, in general, to devote to their responsibilities.

All of their time	
Most (over 50 per cent) of their time	
About a quarter of their time	
Less than a quarter of their time	
Very little (less than 10 per cent) of their time	

2:5 Are teachers in your school, other
than those awarded scale posts,
given responsibility for areas of
work? If 'Yes', please specify for
what they are responsible.

Yes

No

What functions do you expect them to perform?

2:6 In the report of the survey by HM Inspectors of Schools, of primary education in England, it is stated: 'Consideration needs to be given to improving (the) standing of teachers with posts of special responsibility . . . '

How do you consider that an improved standing for teachers with posts of special responsibility might be achieved?

_____

_____

_____

_____

_____

2:7 In your opinion, should it be necessary for teachers given a post of responsibility to undertake a course of training?

Yes ☐

No ☐

If 'Yes', (a) what should be the content of such a course of training?

_____

_____

(b) who should be responsible for the training?

_____

_____

2:8   To whom should post-holders be responsible? (e.g. head, staff meeting etc.)

_____

_____

2:9   How should the exercise of responsibility be monitored?

_____

_____

_____

_____

_____

_____

2:10   Are you generally in agreement with the present practices in appointing teachers to posts of responsibility?

Yes

No

If 'No', please outline what practices in your opinion should be pursued in primary schools in appointing teachers to areas of responsibility; what area of activity and expertise should be involved and in what ways?

_____

_____

_____

_____

Section 3

3:1 In *Primary Education in England: A Survey by H.M. Inspectors of Schools,* it was suggested that one way of making fuller use of teachers' particular strengths would be to make their expertise more generally available by giving them responsibility for an aspect of the curriculum. In this respect they, like their colleagues with paid or special posts of responsibility, would be available to give advice and guidance. It is about the possible effects of using such teacher experts, the areas of the curriculum where their advice and guidance would be welcome and the professional and personal qualities needed to discharge such a role effectively, that this section of the questionnaire is concerned.

What is your opinion of this suggestion?

Is it a) an excellent one?   ☐

    b) a good one generally, but
        posing some difficulties?   ☐

    c) an idea of only limited
        practicality?   ☐

    d) an idea likely to cause
        more harm than good?   ☐

Please tick *one*

Would you say below briefly what prompts you to hold the above opinion.

_____

_____

_____

_____

_____

General Comments:

_____

_____

_____

_____

_____

_____

_____

_____

_____

_____

_____

_____

_____

_____

_____

_____

APPENDIX 3

Teachers' Questionnaire

Section 1

The purpose of this section is to obtain basic biographical information. As with all other sections of the questionnaire, your responses will be treated as entirely confidential. Please tick in the appropriate spaces.

1:1 For how long have you been teaching?

- 0-5 years ☐
- 6-10 years ☐
- 11-15 years ☐
- over 15 years ☐

1:2 Are you . . . . . .

- Male? ☐
- Female? ☐

1:3 Which of the following describes your position in the school?

- Deputy head ☐
- Teacher with a paid post of responsibility ☐
- Teacher with an unpaid post of responsibility ☐
- Teacher ☐

Other (please specify)

....

1:4 Which of the following age group are you presently teaching?

Nursery

Reception

6 +

7 +

8 +

9 +

10 +

11 +

1:5 Which of the following qualifications do you hold?

BEd

Teaching cert.

Postgraduate cert.

BA/BSc

MEd

Advanced diploma

1:6 Are you a member of a teaching association (not a union)? If 'yes' please specify

Yes

No

....

....

....

1:7 To what extent in your view should all primary school teachers have competence in the following curriculum areas: Please use the following scale: Fully: 3, Partially: 2, Not necessary: 1. Please ring as appropriate.

a) Mathematics   3 2 1
b) Reading and language skills   3 2 1
c) Science   3 2 1
d) Music   3 2 1
e) Environmental studies and/or topic work   3 2 1
f) Art and craft   3 2 1
g) Physical education and games   3 2 1
h) Geography, history, social studies   3 2 1
i) Religious education   3 2 1

1:8 In your view, what degree of importance should be attached to *each* of the following as a source of professional development for the primary school teacher in addition to their own professional experience? Please use the following scale and ring as appropriate: Extremely important: 4, Very important: 3, Important: 2, Fairly important: 1

a) Support from the local advisory service or the inspectorate   4 3 2 1
b) Guidance from the head teacher   4 3 2 1
c) Information and suggestions from national reports and surveys   4 3 2 1
d) Support from school-based, in-service courses   4 3 2 1
e) Help from colleagues with special knowledge and experience   4 3 2 1
f) Ideas from the professional literature   4 3 2 1
g) Support from the professional literature   4 3 2 1
h) Help from teachers with scale posts of responsibility   4 3 2 1
i) Ideas from textbooks and teachers' guides   4 3 2 1
j) Help from sympathetic colleagues   4 3 2 1

**THE REMAINDER OF SECTION 1 TO BE COMPLETED
ONLY BY TEACHERS WITH POSTS OF RESPONSIBILITY**

1:9   As a teacher with a post of responsibility, in which of the following areas does your responsibility fall?

a)   Responsibility for teaching a particular subject, e.g. music, PE, reading, science.
Please specify the subject...................

b)   Responsibility for a curriculum area, e.g. language, mathematics etc.
Please specify the area......................

c)   Responsibility for teaching a particular group of children, e.g. those in need of remedial teaching, more able children.
Please specify the group.....................

d)   Responsibility for teaching materials and/or resources, e.g. text or library books.
Please specify..................................

e)   Responsibility for an aspect of school organization or administration, e.g. management of stock, purchase of materials etc.
Please specify aspect.........................

f)   Responsibility for the welfare of children, e.g. pastoral care.
Please specify..................................

IF NONE OF THE ABOVE IS
APPLICABLE PLEASE DESCRIBE
THE AREA OF YOUR
RESPONSIBILITY

g)   ....
....
....

1:10 When you accepted your post of responsibility, were you given an account of the work you were to do:

a) formally?   OR

b) informally?

How was this done?

a) in written form?

b) verbally?

c) in detail?

d) in general terms?

Please tick where applicable

Would you have wished to have more information regarding your responsibilities?

YES

NO

If 'YES' please indicate below the kind of information you would have wished for

....

....

....

....

1:11 How much of your time in school is officially taken up in discharging your responsibilities? (This may be difficult to answer – please give a rough estimate below.)

a) All your time in school

b) Most (over 50 per cent) of your time

c) About a quarter of your time

d) Less than a quarter of your time

e) Very little (less than 10 per cent) of your time

Please tick one

1:12 How much of your *own time* do you spend on activities related to your post of responsibility?
(Please state hours per week)   _____ h.p.w.

1:13 The skills I have as a post holder are used   3 2 1
to their full capacity

(Please use the following scale)
   Very much so   3
   Generally so   2
   Rarely   1

The time I spend as a post-holder is put to   3 2 1
profitable use

Section 2

THIS SECTION SHOULD BE COMPLETED BY ALL TEACHERS

This section seeks to discover those functions and activities that teachers in general think that holders of posts of responsibility, both paid and unpaid, *should* undertake.

For each of the following functions and activities please indicate the extent to which teachers with posts of responsibility *should* be involved

Frequently (i.e. more or less daily)	5
Sometimes (i.e. more or less weekly)	4
Occasionally (i.e. more or less termly)	3
Seldom (i.e. once or twice a year)	2
Not at all	1
e.g. Reading the daily paper	⑤ 4 3 2 1

2:1 *Teaching and curricular responsibilities*

a) Teaching a particular subject to classes that are not 'their own'   5 4 3 2 1

b) Demonstrating a lesson or teaching method for their colleagues   5 4 3 2 1

c) Discussing with colleagues up-to-date methods of teaching a particular subject or area of the curriculum   5 4 3 2 1

d) Teaching a particular class or group of children e.g. reception class, remedial group   5 4 3 2 1

e) Showing colleagues or displaying children's work arising from teaching a particular subject or area of the curriculum   5 4 3 2 1

f) Planning or developing a programme of work for a special group of children e.g. a remedial group, children of high ability   5 4 3 2 1

g) Keeping an eye on work in a particular 5   4   3   2   1
    area of the curriculum e.g. language
    work for lower juniors

h) Assessing the standards of achievement 5   4   3   2   1
    in an area of the curriculum e.g.
    administering a standardized test,
    listening to children read

i) Testing or screening for grouping or 5   4   3   2   1
    setting children.

j) Chairing a group of colleagues to work in 5   4   3   2   1
    an area of the curriculum.

k) Planning a scheme of work in a 5   4   3   2   1
    curriculum area for general use within
    the school e.g. a scheme in
    environmental studies or mathematics.

l) Keeping up-to-date in a particular 5   4   3   2   1
    subject or in relation to a particular
    group of children e.g. by reading recent
    accounts of relevant work, studies or
    reports.

m) Supervising the work of other teachers 5   4   3   2   1
    e.g. probationers or students on
    practice.

n) Teaching children whose first language is 5   4   3   2   1
    not English, e.g. immigrant children.

2:2 *Resource responsibilities*

a) Maintaining and developing teaching 5   4   3   2   1
    resources in an area of the curriculum for
    general use in the school.

b) Ordering materials, books etc. for an 5   4   3   2   1
    area of teaching on behalf of colleagues.

c) Organizing reprographic facilities for 5   4   3   2   1
    use by colleagues e.g. duplicated
    teaching materials.

d) Managing library books and other 5   4   3   2   1
    resources.

e) Maintaining a specialist room or facility 5   4   3   2   1
    for colleagues.

2:3 *Welfare and liaison responsibilities*

   a) Liaising on behalf of the school with   5 4 3 2 1
infant or secondary school.

   b) Looking after the welfare of children on   5 4 3 2 1
behalf of the school e.g. pastoral care.

   c) Liaising with parents on behalf of the   5 4 3 2 1
school.

   d) Liaising with agencies such as the LEA,   5 4 3 2 1
Children's Department or the Child
Psychological Service on behalf of the
school.

   e) Caring for children hurt or ill during   5 4 3 2 1
school hours.

2:4 *Administrative and organizing*
responsibilities

   a) Administering an aspect of the work of   5 4 3 2 1
the school office

   b) Organizing an event for the school e.g.   5 4 3 2 1
parents' evening, meeting of the PTA
etc.

   c) Organizing an event for a group of   5 4 3 2 1
children on behalf of colleagues e.g. a
school visit.

2:5 *Other responsibilities*
Please state below responsibilities not
covered above, and rate them.

   a) 5 4 3 2 1

     ....

   b) 5 4 3 2 1

     ....

   c) 5 4 3 2 1

     ....

Section 3

In *Primary Education in England: A Survey by H.M. Inspectors of Schools,* It was suggested that one way of making fuller use of teachers' particular strengths would be to make their expertise more generally available by giving them responsibility for an aspect of the curriculum. In this respect they, like their colleagues with paid or special posts of responsibility, would be available to give advice and guidance. It is about the possible effects of using more widely the expertise of teachers, the areas of the curriculum where their advice and guidance would be welcome and the professional and personal qualities needed by teachers making more widely available their expertise, that this section of the questionnaire is concerned.

In places the term 'expert' has been used as an abbreviation for 'the use of teacher expertise'.

3:1   In which of the following curriculum areas do you think that class teachers would wish to draw from the expertise of other teachers. Please use the following scale:

Very much   3
To some extent   2
Not at all   1

And please be sure to enter a rating on
every line under each column.

Curriculum area	Preparing schemes of work	Advising on teaching methods	Advising on methods of assessment	Managing resources
Mathematics				
Science				
History, geog. soc. studies				
Religious Education				
Music				
Language & reading skills				
Art & craft				
Environmental studies & topic work				
PE & games				

3:2 Please indicate the extent to which you agree with the following statements about the nature of teaching in primary schools and the possible effects of introducing the wider use of the expertise of teachers. Please use the following scale, completing all items:

Very much agree	5	Please circle
Agree	4	appropriate
Neither agree		number
nor disagree	3	
Disagree	2	
Strongly disagree	1	

a) The only basis for sound education in the primary school is class teaching. 5 4 3 2 1

b) The teacher with responsibility for a curriculum area is essential to sound educational practices in the primary school. 5 4 3 2 1

c) Class teaching is the best way to get to know how children learn and so be able to help them. 5 4 3 2 1

d) No class teacher can expect to be able to cover *all* areas of the curriculum and so provide an effective education. 5 4 3 2 1

e) Class teaching provides the child with the kind of security and confidence that facilitates learning. 5 4 3 2 1

f) Only under the guidance of an 'expert' is it possible for children to understand certain areas of the curriculum. 5 4 3 2 1

g) The teacher with special responsibility for a curriculum area is an essential resource in the primary school. 5 4 3 2 1

h) A change of teachers unsettles the primary school child and makes him less able to learn. 5 4 3 2 1

i) All teachers in the primary school have special teaching talents and every effort should be made to use these throughout the school. 5 4 3 2 1

j) Teachers in the primary school welcome 5 4 3 2 1 help in areas of teaching where they are weak.

k) Class teachers in the primary school 5 4 3 2 1 need help and advice in planning schemes of work.

l) There is scope in the primary school for 5 4 3 2 1 teachers who have responsibility for teaching a subject rather than a class.

m) The continuity of relationship with one 5 4 3 2 1 teacher is a necessary feature of sound primary education.

n) Without some teacher specialization in 5 4 3 2 1 the primary school its curriculum would be unbalanced.

o) Class teaching is essential to ensure 5 4 3 2 1 curriculum coordination and continuity.

p) Class teaching is necessary if day-to-day 5 4 3 2 1 adjustments of the curriculum are to take place.

q) Teachers will ask advice of someone 5 4 3 2 1 with a clearly designated curriculum expertise.

r) Teachers are more inclined to seek 5 4 3 2 1 information about the curriculum than advice on teaching it.

s) Informal (rather than formal) contact 5 4 3 2 1 between teachers facilitates the asking and giving of advice.

t) Class teachers cannot be expected to 5 4 3 2 1 cover all the areas of the primary school curriculum with equal confidence.

u) Specialist teaching in the primary school 5 4 3 2 1 is the only way that all aspects of the curriculum can be covered adequately.

v) Specialist teaching in the primary school 5 4 3 2 1 will lead to the fragmentation of learning.

w) Cooperation between teachers and 5 4 3 2 1 team-teaching are adequate substitutes for specialist teaching in the primary school.

x) It would be sensible to abolish posts of 5 4 3 2 1
    responsibility in primary schools and
    share duties equitably among the staff.

y) The idea of posts of responsibility in the 5 4 3 2 1
    primary school is directly opposed to
    the ideal of professional responsibility
    to which every teacher should aspire.

z) Posts of responsibility in primary 5 4 3 2 1
    schools provide a very good opportunity
    to develop the skills necessary if one is
    to seek promotion.

3:3 If primary school teachers are to make more widely available
     their expertise, in which of the following curriculum areas
     and activities do you believe that primary school teachers will
     have expertise to offer? Please use the following scale and
     please complete all items.

A great deal   5   Please ring
A considerable amount   4   as
A fair amount   3   appropriate
Something   2
Little or nothing   1

a) Knowledge in a particular academic 5 4 3 2 1
    subject

b) Practical experience of the classroom 5 4 3 2 1

c) Understanding human relations   5 4 3 2 1

d) Management and administrative skills   5 4 3 2 1

e) Technical know-how with visual and 5 4 3 2 1
    other aids

f) Understanding the philosophy of 5 4 3 2 1
    primary education

g) Knowledge of child psychology   5 4 3 2 1

h) Knowledge of social relations in school 5 4 3 2 1
    and classrooms

i) Competence and experience in a 5 4 3 2 1
    leadership role

j) Understanding of teaching techniques   5 4 3 2 1

k) Skills needed for developing schemes of   5   4   3   2   1
    work
l) Knowledge of the theory of teaching   5   4   3   2   1
m) Skills in debate and discussion   5   4   3   2   1
n) Organizational skills   5   4   3   2   1
o) Knowledge of how children learn   5   4   3   2   1
p) Skills needed for the successful handling   5   4   3   2   1
    of meetings, working parties etc.
q) Experience of curriculum development   5   4   3   2   1
    work
r) Experience of teaching at more than   5   4   3   2   1
    one level of education e.g. primary *and*
    secondary

3:4   Please indicate the extent to which you agree with the
      following statements about how the teacher 'expert' should
      function.
      Please use the scale below, completing all items.

Very much agree   5   Please ring
Agree   4   as
Neither agree nor disagree 3   appropriate
Disagree   2
Strongly disagree   1

a) The teacher 'expert' should discharge   5   4   3   2   1
    his function in the best interests of the
    school in which he works.
b) It is important that the teacher 'expert'   5   4   3   2   1
    discharges his function in the best
    interests of primary education.
c) In discharging his function the teacher   5   4   3   2   1
    'expert' should bear in mind the
    recommendations of national reports on
    primary ed.
d) The prime concern of the teacher   5   4   3   2   1
    'expert' should be the educational
    interests of the children in the school in
    which he works.
e) It is important that the teacher 'expert'   5   4   3   2   1
    discharges his function so that he

        contributes to the professional development of his immediate colleagues.

f) The teacher 'expert' must be constantly 5 4 3 2 1 aware of innovations in primary schooling introduced by such national organizations as the Schools Council.

g) The teacher 'expert' should focus his 5 4 3 2 1 attention on desirable changes in teaching in the school in which he works

h) The teacher 'expert' should concentrate 5 4 3 2 1 on his area of responsibility within the school to the exclusion of all others.

i) The teacher 'expert' should extend his 5 4 3 2 1 field of interest in subjects other than his own, and in other aspects of the curriculum.

j) The teacher 'expert' should be prepared 5 4 3 2 1 to share his specialist knowledge and skills with his colleagues.

k) The teacher 'expert' should be able to 5 4 3 2 1 accept suggestions and criticism from colleagues about his methods.

3:5 On which of the following would depend – in your view – the efficient use of the teacher 'expert' in the primary school, and to what extent?

Please use the following key:

To a great extent	3	Please ring
To some extent	2	as
Not at all	1	appropriate

a) The status which they are accorded by   3 2 1 other teachers.

b) The *time in school* that they are able to   3 2 1 devote to their duties rather than teach.

c) The extent to which they can be freed from   3 2 1 teaching to attend courses.

d) The length and relevance of their own   3 2 1 teaching experience.

e)   The degree of access they have to the head   3 2 1
     and other senior staff.

f)   The time they can give *out of school* to   3 2 1
     their responsibilities.

g)   The extent to which they are given   3 2 1
     secretarial and other support.

h)   The extent to which they have resources,   3 2 1
     both financial and material on which to
     draw.

i)   The degree to which the sphere of   3 2 1
     responsibility is clear and explicit.

j)   The degree to which the school has   3 2 1
     thought through its aims and objectives.

k)   The emphasis the school gives to the   3 2 1
     monitoring and assessment of standards.

l)   The degree of support they receive from   3 2 1
     the head and other senior staff.

4:1 If training for posts of responsibility is necessary, in which of
     the following fields should training be required?
     Please tick those which you think apply:

a)   personal relationships

b)   knowledge of a curriculum area

c)   child psychology

d)   organization/administration

e)   environmental studies

f)   remedial work

g)   transition to secondary education

h)   high ability children

i)   assessment of children's capabilities

j)   knowledge of diagnostic tests

4:2 In your view, what might a policy to encourage the use of
     teacher 'experts' in the primary school result in?
     Please answer all items and use the following scale:

Very likely	4	Please ring
Likely	3	as
Unlikely	2	appropriate
Very unlikely	1	

a) The erosion of class teaching 4 3 2 1
b) Higher standards of teaching all round 4 3 2 1
c) A general rise in the morale of staff 4 3 2 1
d) A fragmentation of children's curricular experience 4 3 2 1
e) Higher standards only in the basic subjects 4 3 2 1
f) An increase in morale *only* of those teachers designated 'expert' 4 3 2 1
g) An improved educational base for primary schools 4 3 2 1
h) A fairer distribution of teaching resources 4 3 2 1
i) A greater economy of teaching resources 4 3 2 1
j) The readier control of the primary school curriculum by the LEA and the state 4 3 2 1
k) Lack of balance in the curriculum 4 3 2 1
l) Greater demand by teachers in the primary school for in-service courses 4 3 2 1
m) Less job satisfaction for primary school teachers 4 3 2 1
n) Less matching of the individual child and what learning is required 4 3 2 1

The space below is for any comments you might have regarding this questionnaire, or aspects of your job which you feel have not been covered on the preceding pages:

_____

_____

_____

_____

_____

APPENDIX 4

Factor Analysis Of Teachers' Opinions Of Likely Effect Of A Wider Use Of Teacher Expertise

Factor analysis: what it is

Factor analysis is a mathematical technique for reducing a large and complex number of responses or ratings to the lowest, simplest number possible.

If we inspect the responses of all the teachers to all the questions (or statements) in one of the sections of the questionnaire, we find that in many instances the teachers will respond differently; some will 'agree' with the question (or statement), while others will 'disagree'. We might ask: are the differences in the teachers' responses systematic or are they specifically related to the particular question (or statement) to which they have responded? Factor analysis helps us to hazard a useful guess at an answer. Each substantial factor which a factor analysis produces may be thought of as a systematic stance to or a perception of an issue contained within a collection of questions (or statements). An example may help. If we were to ask a sample of people to answer questions on the kinds of food which they liked, a factor analysis might well show two major food preferences: one showing a preference for 'sweet' foods and one showing a preference for 'savoury' foods. Similarly it was in order to show the basis of teachers' perceptions about a range of effects on them and on the primary school, and aspects of its organization of the use of teacher experts that the following factor analyses were carried out.

Section 3:2

Effects of introducing wider use of teacher experts in the primary school on the nature of teaching

Factor 1

Item: o) Class teaching is essential to ensure   0.814
curriculum coordination and continuity.

p) Class teaching is necessary if day to day   0.729
adjustments of the curriculum are to take
place.

m) The continuity of relationship with one   0.434
teacher is a necessary feature of sound
primary education.

a) The only basis for sound education in the   0.429
primary school is class teaching.
Percentage Variance 30.6

Description

The factor reflects belief in the value of class teaching and curriculum continuity. It is this that teachers see being affected by the introduction of a wider use of teacher experts.

Factor 2

Item: u) Specialist teaching in the primary school is +0.718
the only way that all aspects of the curriculum
can be covered adequately.

i)   There is scope in the primary school for +0.481
teaching a subject rather than a class.

n) Without some teacher specialization in the +0.421
primary school its curriculum would be
unbalanced.

v) Specialist teaching in the primary school will −0.575
lead to the fragmentation of learning.

w) Cooperation between teachers and −0.499
team-teaching are adequate substitutes for
specialist teaching in the primary school.
Percentage Variance 29.5

Description

This is a bi-polar factor in which a positive and negative
perspective are shown together as opposite ends of a scale. The
scale is concerned with the presumed effects of specialist teaching
in the primary school resulting from the introduction of the wider
use of teacher experts.

Factor 3

Item: x) It would be sensible to abolish posts of 0.0875
responsibility in the primary school and share
duties equitably among the staff.
y) The idea of posts of responsibility in the 0.855
primary school is directly opposed to the ideal
of professional responsibility to which every
teacher should aspire.
Percentage Variance 13.1

Description

The factor is a limited one concerned with the possible effect on
special posts of responsibility.

Summary

The erosion of the values of class, and the risk of subject-teaching
are brought out as possible effects of the wider use of teacher
experts in the primary school, at least as perspectives from which
to view potential consequences by the responding teachers. In a
slighter way the possible effects on posts of special responsibility
are silhouetted.

Section 3:3

The areas of the curriculum in which teachers will have expertise to offer

Factor 1

Item:
g)	Knowledge of child psychology	0.769
f)	Understanding the philosophy of primary education	0.749
l)	Knowledge of the theory of teaching	0.644
h)	Knowledge of social relations in schools and classrooms	0.600
o)	Knowledge of how children learn	0.432
m)	Skills in debate and discussion	0.421
	Percentage Variance	72.7

Description

This is a much smaller factor than the previous one, and collects together expertise in managerial and practical skills and experience outside the classroom.

Factor 3

Item:
j)	Understanding of teaching techniques	0.685
k)	Skills needed for developing schemes of work	0.559
o)	Knowledge of how children learn	0.505
	Percentage Variance	7.0

Description

This is a slight factor which may refer to classroom related expertise. But this is clearly an uncertain description.

Summary

It would seem that teachers see as the most likely expertise to be made available by colleagues to be that of their professional knowledge and understanding. The other kind of expertise seen as most likely to be made available by their colleagues is that involving managerial and practical skills and experience.

Section 3:4

How Should the Teacher Expert Function?

Factor 1	*Loading*

Item: f) The teacher expert must be constantly aware   .758
of innovation in primary schooling introduced
by such national organizations as the Schools
Council.

    g) The teacher expert should focus his attention   .509
on desirable changes in teaching in the school
in which he works.

    c) In discharging his function the teacher expert   .480
should bear in mind the recommendation of
national reports.

    d) It is important that the teacher expert   .441
discharges his function so that he contributes
to the professional development of his
immediate colleagues.

        Percentage Variance 68.0

Description

This factor shows the teacher expert as an agent of change, alert to innovations in primary education and making a signal contribution to the professional growth of his colleagues.

Factor 2		*Loading*

Item: a) The teacher expert should discharge his function in the best interests of the school in which he works. — 0.636

b) The teacher expert should discharge his function in the best interests of primary education. — 0.561

d) The prime concern of the teacher expert should be the educational interests of the children in the school in which he works. — 0.433

c) In discharging his function the teacher expert should bear in mine the recommendations of national reports on primary education. — 0.415

Percentage Variance 21.3

Description

'Concern' appears to be the key word in describing this 'teacher expert'; concern for the educational well being of all involved in primary education. The description is more about a stance to be adopted by the teacher expert than about his functioning.

Summary

Two reasonably clear views of how the teacher expert might function emerge in this analysis. The first is of the teacher expert as an agent of change: an innovator. The second, as a concerned colleague – concerned for the well-being of the school in which he works, and its children. Concerned also with primary education in general. The role of the innovative teacher expert is likely to have a cosmopolitan outlook. That of the concerned teacher expert is likely to be more parochial.

Section 4:2

Results of a policy encouraging the use of teacher experts

Factor 1	*Loading*

Item:

n) Less matching of the individual child and what learning is required — 0.708

k) Lack of balance in the curriculum — 0.664

m) Less job satisfaction for primary school teachers — 0.628

d) A fragmentation of a child's curricular experience — 0.578

a) The erosion of class teaching — 0.563

f) An increase in *morale* only of those teachers designated 'expert' — 0.548

j) The readier control of the primary school curriculum by the LEA and the State — 0.413

Percentage Variance . . . . — 11.3

Description

This factor collects together all the possible negative effects of a policy which encourages the use of teacher experts in the primary school.

Factor 2	*Loading*

Item:

b) Higher standards of teaching all round — 0.741

c) A general rise in morale of the staff — 0.627

g) An improved educational base for primary schools — 0.526

l) A greater demand by teachers in the primary school for in-service courses — 0.395

Percentage Variance . . . . — 12.5

Description

This factor is the opposite of Factor 1 in collecting together all the perceived *positive* effects of a policy of encouraging the use of teacher experts in the primary school.

Factor 3

Item:			
	h)	A fairer distribution of teaching loads within the primary school	0.738
	i)	A greater economy of teaching resources	0.583
	g)	An improved educational base for primary schools	0.397
		Percentage Variance	6.2

Description

This is a very small factor and only a tentative interpretation of it can be made. It could possibly be to do with the managerial effects of the introduction of a perceived policy to encourage the use of teacher experts.

Summary

It is not surprising that some teachers see negative effects arising from the implementation of a policy to encourage the use of teacher experts in the primary school, and others see positive effects. These would appear from the factor analysis to be the two major perspectives from which to view a policy to encourage the use of teacher experts. A third perspective – managerial effects – is much less sure.

APPENDIX 5

Brief For Groups – Teacher Expert In The Primary School

1. The following are the main questions to which the groups should address themselves:

   What is a 'teacher expert' in the primary school?

   What function should be assigned to the teacher expert in the primary school?

   How should a teacher expert be used in the primary school?

   What kind of training, if any, should a teacher expert receive?

   How may their expertise be improved?

2. Each group should appoint a chairman and an observer, and make arrangements for their discussions to be taped.
3. The observer should keep an account of each meeting and make an analysis of its deliberations.
4. The group may appoint a secretary to keep notes or minutes, and if required, an agenda for meetings.
5. Groups should expect to meet on some six to ten occasions.
6. Each group will produce a report.

APPENDIX 6

Primary Schools Research And Development Group – Free Account of Teacher Experts

Section A

Please underline the most appropriate answers, unless stated otherwise. Please do not omit any question in this section.

Scale	1; 2; 3; 4; Deputy Head
Sex	Male Female
Number of years in teaching	0-5 6-10 Over 10 years
Own class	Yes/No (if class teacher state which age group you teach)

Previous teaching experience

Please state the types of school in which you have taught.

Area of responsibility

What is your area of responsibility? Please specify

Section B

Role descriptions

In this section you are asked to give a written account of your role in your area/areas of responsibility. Please provide details of what your role of responsibility is likely to involve during the school year (September to July). It is hoped that you will also describe some of your rewards and frustrations in fulfilling this role:

APPENDIX 7

Diary Instructions

Please record under the following headings those actions and events and decisions that are concerned with your area of 'specialism or responsibility'.

Planning:
includes responsibility for schemes, advice on choice of activity or topic associated with your specialism, advice on structuring 'instruction', discussion with head teacher about possible direction work might take, resources, etc., attendance at conferences, courses, visits to other schools.

Resources:
responsibility for ordering books, materials, apparatus etc., responsibility for maintaining the above, advice on choice of resources.

Displays:
advising on displays, special responsibility for particular displays, e.g. Harvest Festival, new books. Drawing together items for information for others e.g. colleagues, governors, tutors.

Advising:
advising students on teaching practice, advising probationer teachers, initiating staff meetings on the 'specialism'.

Teaching/testing:
responsibility for screening children or testing, responsibility for teaching other classes or groups of children.

Other activities:
any items that are seasonal and that you have not been able to include as they occur at certain times of the year may be entered here, any other items you wish to include. (These may all be entered at the rear of the diary.)

Publications Consulted

BASSEY, M. (1978). *Nine Hundred Primary School Teachers*. Windsor: NFER-NELSON.

BECHER, T. *et al.* (1981). *Policies for Educational Accountability*. London: Heinemann.

BERGER, P.L., BERGER, R. and KELLNER, H. (1973). *The Homeless Mind*. Harmondsworth: Penguin Books.

BERLACK, A. and H. (1981). *Dilemmas of Schooling*. London: Methuen.

BETTLEHEIM, B. and ZELAND, K. (1982). *On Learning to Read: The Child's Fascination with Meaning*. New York: Knopf.

BOARD OF EDUCATION (1918). *Handbook of Suggestions for Teachers*. London: HMSO.

BOARD OF EDUCATION (1927). *Handbook for Teachers*. London: HMSO.

BORGHI, L. (1974). *Perspectives in Primary Education*. The Hague: Martinus Nijhoff.

BOULDING, K. (1985). *Human Betterment*. London: Sage Publications.

BOYD, J. (1984). *Understanding the Primary Curriculum*. London: Hutchinson.

BRENNAN, E.J.T. (Ed) (1975). *Education for National Efficiency*. London: Athlone Press.

BUSSIE, A.M., CHITTENDEN, E.A. and AMAREL, M. (1970). *Beyond Surface Curriculum*. Boulder, Colorado: Westview Press.

COOPER, D.E. (1983). *Authenticity and Learning*. London: Routledge & Kegan Paul.

DEPARTMENT OF EDUCATION AND SCIENCE (1959). *Primary Education*. London: HMSO.

DEPARTMENT OF EDUCATION AND SCIENCE (1984). *Report by HMIs on effects of Local Authority Expenditure Policies on Education Provision in England, 1983*. London: Department of Education and Science.

GORDON, P. and LAWTON, D. (1978). *Curriculum Change in the Nineteenth and Twentieth Centuries*. London: Hodder and Stoughton.

GOWIN, D.B. (1981). *Educating*. London: Cornell University Press.

GRAFF, H. (1979). *The Literacy Myth*. London: Academic Press.

GRAFF, H. (Ed) (1981). *Literacy and Social Development in the West.* Cambridge: Cambridge University Press.

KIRBY, N. (1981). *Personal Values in Primary Education.* London: Harper Row.

LOWNDES, G.A.N. (1969). *The Silent Social Revolution,* 2nd Edition. Oxford University Press.

MACLURE, J.S. (1979). *Educational Documents: England and Wales 1816 to the Present Day.* London: Methuen.

MAUSE, LLOYD DE (Ed). (1974) *The History of Childhood.* London: Souvenir Press, (E & A) Ltd.

MINISTRY OF EDUCATION (1944). *Handbook of Suggestions for Teachers.* London: HMSO.

MUSGROVE, F. (1982). *Education and Anthropology: Other Cultures and the Teacher.* London: John Wiley.

OECD (1983). *Compulsory Schooling in a Changing World.* Paris: OECD.

RICHARDS, C. (1984). *The Study of Primary Education: A Source Book Volume 1.* Lewes: Falmer Press.

SCHOOLS COUNCIL (1983). *Primary Practice.* London: Methuen Educational.

SELLECK, R.J.W. (1968). *The New Education.* London: Pitman and Sons.

SELLECK, R.J.W. (1972). *English Primary Education and the Progressives 1914-1939.* London: Routledge & Kegan Paul.

SIMON, B. (1980). 'The Primary School Revolution; Myth or Reality?' in *History of Education Society. Proceedings of the Annual Conference.*

STEPHENS, J.M. (1967). *The Process of Schooling.* London: Holt, Rinehart and Winston.

WALLER, W. (1932). *The Sociology of Teacher.* New York: John Wiley.

WRIGHT, N. (1977). *Progress in Education.* London: Croom Helm.

Author Index

Subject Index